MILITARY INSTITUTIONS AND POWER
IN THE NEW STATES

By the same author
ARMED FORCES IN THE NEW STATES

William Gutteridge

MILITARY
INSTITUTIONS
AND POWER IN
THE NEW STATES

FREDERICK A. PRAEGER, Publishers
NEW YORK · WASHINGTON · LONDON

FREDERICK A. PRAEGER, *Publishers*
111 Fourth Avenue, New York 3, N.Y., U.S.A.
77-79 Charlotte Street, London W.1, England

Published in the United States of America in 1965
by Frederick A. Praeger, Inc., Publishers

© William Gutteridge 1965
Library of Congress Catalog Card Number: 65-12441

Printed in Great Britain

CONTENTS

Preface

IN THIS BOOK I HAVE attempted to examine the nature of the armed forces in the newly independent states, their role in the societies from which they derive and the influence which they tend to exert internally and on international relations. A really comprehensive study of this subject would involve an examination in depth of the political and social structure of most of the countries to which reference is made: this is clearly beyond the capacity of a single individual, but it has seemed worthwhile in this case to attempt the task, drawing examples from as wide a field as possible. The result inevitably is uneven: a few topics and states are dealt with at length, others superficially. Ireland, in spite of her technical 'newness' and her participation in the United Nations force in the Congo, has been omitted because of the closeness of her association with the developed European tradition. Another limiting factor affecting the selection of material has been the deliberate obscurity which is preserved in some countries with regard to the most element-ary military facts; I have had to draw on the normally accessible sources and thus the reliability of information is not always certain.

The initial impetus for an investigation of this subject derived from a Nuffield Travelling Fellowship in 1960–61, but the present work is largely the result of fresh research over the last eighteen months. I am, however, most grateful to Mr Philip Mason, Director of the Institute of Race Relations, for permission to draw heavily on material previously published for that institute by Oxford University Press, in my own short book, *Armed Forces in New States*, and in articles in the journal *Race*.

I should also like to acknowledge the invaluable assistance of those who typed the manuscript against time and, in particular, of Mrs Angela Thompson who set the high standard achieved. The book would, however, never have been completed had it not been for the tolerance and encouragement of my wife and daughters at weekends during the winter months of 1963–64.

June 1964   *W. F. G.*

I

Independence and the New Elites

THE ACHIEVEMENT OF INDEPENDENCE is not an abrupt process by which overnight a former colony becomes a new state holding its rightful place in the community of nations: it is in most cases, in practice, a long drawn-out evolution in which many of the essential institutions are almost imperceptibly modified in preparation for the event or adapted to meet the new circumstances after the formalities have taken place. The time scale, of course, varies: as the twentieth century has progressed, the scale has tended to telescope. But even this apparently simple statement of an historical truth can be misleading, for the longer the period over which power is in the process of transference pre-independence, the shorter may be the subsequent period of adaptation. It might well be argued that at the moment of independence Indian national institutions were more clearly defined than those of Nigeria at the corresponding time, and that Nigeria in October 1960 was further developed in this respect than was Tanganyika in December 1961.

The process of independence has a number of phases and in few new states is the final stage nearing completion. Clearly, where the political leadership is forceful and effective, the period immediately following the achievement of independence sees the most rapid development, amounting to a crescendo of activity after a period of gradual change inevitably restrained in some degree by the colonial power. The extent of this restraint is affected by early or late recognition of the vision of self-government. The majority of French-speaking African countries, whose national institutions are developing very slowly, had little time to experience the approach of independence before it was nominally upon them and, because of the nature of the economic and military relationship with France, have yet to suffer or enjoy its full reality.

According to their place in the structure of society and the attitudes of the political leaders towards them, the various institutions and activities of the state conform in some measure to the general process. In the first place, because it is the symbol of freedom, the constitutional structure is the main subject of attention; without some drastic change there is no independence, though in British territories apparently viable government machinery has often been a pre-condition of the lifting of the imperial yoke. The concept of 'trusteeship' has resulted in tutelary government in what has been conceived to be the best interest of the community at large. The needs of embryonic new states may have been misinterpreted, partly because no imperial power can be expected to use as criteria of adequacy other systems than its own, but the intentions have been of the best. This type of historical circumstance, directly reflecting the character of the specific imperialism, has a clear bearing on the evolutionary process as a whole. It may well determine the extent of the revolutionary reaction to it.

The comparative speed of change as between, for instance, the civil service, the police, the education system and the army is affected by many factors. The cry of 'Indianization', 'Africanization' or 'localization', or whatever other bastard terminology may be used, is governed in its intensity by pride and sometimes by fear on the part of the politicians, and even in the last resort by the conservatism or otherwise of the particular institution inherited from the guardian foreign power. European armies can safely be described as inherently conservative and they have tended to create in their own images the colonial defence forces out of which national armies have to grow. In Commonwealth countries an apolitical legacy is still apparent, and has indeed in some sense been encouraged by politicians like Kwame Nkrumah and Julius Nyerere who are alert to the dangers of the development of cohesive political consciousness in their officer corps. This has itself induced at times a certain cautiousness towards Africanization in this field, but these scruples have been overwhelmed by the need to nationalize for the sake of the appearance of full freedom in the eyes of fellow 'positive neutrals'. The late Pandit Nehru in altogether different circumstances sought, generally with success, to protect his army against political interference. But whether one looks at the military, or the police, or even, outside the public services, at commerce, the key to the nature of independence is clear—it is the emergence of a leadership elite, necessarily fairly small and compact, which is the most important factor in the political and social development of new states. This is, in the 1960s, the source of power, or at least of profound influence, and in only a few countries in Asia has it any substantial traditional roots. Paradoxically, imperial rule tended to breed its own enemies and, having taken power from one group, has recognized the need to transfer it back to another. These elites are generally Western orientated through the process of education and may be divorced from the harsh realities of mass existence in their own communities. This does not always happen, because they are small in numbers—and not necessarily in political power—but without them the machinery of government, in particular, could not pretend to be indigenous. Because of their restricted dimensions, they tend by nature to be oligarchically inclined, though they have a vested interest in the forms of democracy. Their nature and their relationship with traditional authority, their attitudes and characteristic behaviour form the essential background against which any essay on the military in new states must be set.

A distinction can first be made between Africa and Asia. In Asia, European dominance was never complete and the Western impact comparatively weak. By 1947, the influence of British rule left in a village in Northern Burma or in the Ganges valley in India was relatively superficial. In Africa, the effect of a short period of foreign rule was more intense and, because it was confined almost entirely within the span of the twentieth century with all its technological resources, probably more lasting.

3

Africa was not, as used to be supposed, a *tabula rasa*, but the resistance to change of its own institutions was markedly less than it was in the long established countries of South Asia. Even in Africa, for obvious reasons, the effect of colonial rule was felt irregularly: the coast, as in the Gold Coast, was deeply impregnated with foreign influence, but the interior, especially where Islam was strong, as in Northern Nigeria and what is now Mali, was only lightly tinted. Ideas on politics and education thus took root unevenly, though under British rule the policy was more or less constant in all territories in Africa and Asia, with a stress on political representation on a very gradually increasing scale. The French, on the other hand, while recognizing Africans and Asians as potential Frenchmen, made little progress on the political side towards self-government until the introduction of elections to the Territorial Assemblies in 1946. It is worth noting in this context that French 'colons' in Algeria, Dutch residents in Indonesia, and British settlers in Kenya and Rhodesia constituted an effective check on political representation for the local people and in this and other ways on the rise of a responsible native elite.

Of more general importance than resident European interests was the existence of strong traditional authorities in many areas. Though the group from whom the tribal rulers might be chosen was often fairly wide, those who stood definitely outside it were bound to feel the chill wind of frustration as soon as they were conscious of their own potentialities. Sir George Taubman Goldie, writing in 1898 with special reference to the Nigerian experience, said:[1]

> Yet it is desirable that considerable districts in suitable localities should be administered on European principles by European officials, partly to serve as types to which the native governments may gradually approximate, but principally as cities of refuge in which individuals of more advanced views may find a living, if native government presses unduly upon them; just as, in Europe of the Middle Ages, men whose love of freedom found the iron-bound system of feudalism intolerable sought eagerly the comparative liberty of cities.

[1] Sir George Taubman Goldie, in introduction to S. Vandeleur, *Campaigning on the Upper Nile and Niger* (1898), p. xxiii, quoted in *From Empire to Commonwealth* by Jack Simmons, Odhams, London, 1950, p. 186.

Thus, in a real sense, the spread of European influence served to liberate the energies of a new section of the community, the result of random selection by the educational institutions, usually Christian in origin, through which they passed. The mere fact that in Northern Nigeria administration was mostly in the hands of the Emirs and their officers illustrates the inhibitions inherent in native authority rule; these were also reinforced by the inevitable resistance to Westernization in Islamic communities. It is an ironic commentary on this situation that in Northern Nigeria today, as rivalry with other regions tends to intensify, prominent individuals can be heard to say that they wished Lugard had forced Western education on them in the 1920s. For reasons which vary from area to area, competition between the chiefs and the new generation of educated men was inevitable, with the former gradually giving ground, sometimes because they had abused their authority and undermined their own privileged position. Often, as in the Ivory Coast early in the century, they were caught between the demands of the colonial power and the aspirations or resistance to administrative measures of their own people.

The new elites have carried on the struggle against traditionalism fortified by their own purpose and a new vision of the world. The extent to which Asians, and more particularly Africans, who have acquired education by long and laborious processes, are capable of radical rethinking of their destiny is often underestimated. The visionary nature of Kwame Nkrumah's frequent pronouncements, unrealistic though they often seem, as, for instance, to his fellow Africans at the Addis Ababa Summit Conference in May 1963, evoke a widespread response from young men in the Afro-Asian world. For this, presumably, the intensification of Western educational systems in these countries can claim some responsibility. That the agencies responsible have been and still are largely Christian is also significant. The dictum that the gospel of the New Testament in this environment is a revolutionary doctrine is not the cliché which it seems to have become. Aspirations and mode of education have combined to put a premium on employment of an intellectual nature. The elites in new states are fundamentally those that have the education qualifications combined with the desire to fill that role. The second world war gave them their bearings; in Asia, the defeat of European powers at the hands of the Japanese, and in Africa, military and other experience involving encounters with different societies provided the inspiration for the emergence of nationalist elites. They became revolutionaries though the violence of their revolt varied with the need, with the resistance of the colonial powers to their suddenly articulate demands.

On the whole, African elites have absorbed Western ideas more fully than those of Asia. Some reasons for this have been indicated already, but there is also the fact of the long Asian struggles for independence compared with the brief, almost perfunctory processes of the 1950s and 1960s in Africa. African communities have, therefore, accepted more readily the essentially Western objective of 'modernization'. The elite has been actively concerned to displace the traditional way of life wherever it can be described as primitive. The deprecatory tones of a young Ghanaian from the former Northern Territories, giving a short talk on a subject of his own choice, namely, 'Nudity in the North', illustrated effectively to the author not only the impact of propaganda but a real desire to be 'with it' in the modern world. Such sentiments might be heard in Asia but official endorsement would rarely be categorical. On the other hand, the influence of the Indian National Congress on the African elites has been strong in other ways—notably in the attitude to indiscriminate violence as a political weapon.

An interesting contrast between Asian and African elites of especial importance in the military field, is that in countries like India a large proportion of those seeking professional or political careers have been born to privilege in one form or another. Their contacts have thus often been naturally with their social counterparts in European society. In Africa, the 'upstarts' have had greater success and, though they have adopted the advantages of privilege, such as residence in what were exclusive European areas, have perhaps had less controlled and narrow social experiences. This amounts to a particular indication of a general truth, that emergent African elites seek leadership from amongst their own kind and do not look for some form of 'aristocratic' guidance. They are determined to make a mark on the world in a way which suggests a sense of inferiority derived from the sort of Western contempt for their institutions and culture which, on the whole, Asians have not had to tolerate.

Common to both continents has been a process of separation of the elite from the masses. The very nature of the British educational tradition in particular is such as to tend to create a ruling caste, albeit one into which the products of colonial schools have readily slid. The schools were in many cases created to meet the bureaucratic needs of the administration and their products were inspired by the urge to take it over. Perhaps the additional detachment, indeed isolation, apparent in European military elites is not so easily capable of reproduction: nevertheless it is a significant fact that ready recruiting to their counterparts in Africa and Asia has coincided with overproduction of school-leavers for other purposes and the filling up of professions of comparable status.

The process by which the elite emerges to prominence can be thus traced without much difficulty; it is harder to discover the amalgam of intellectual attitudes which provides its driving force. In the first place, as Western knowledge permeates, it tends to undermine the traditional views of human existence; the most important effect is probably a growing consciousness of the possibility that man may have some control over his own destiny. This in itself is destructive of the essentially magical aspect of the chief's role in Africa; the possibility that reason may be made the main force in human affairs is as revolutionary as the doctrine of equality. All over the newly independent world the avowedly secular has tended to replace the direction of one or more divinities. This is part of an incomplete rejection of the traditional which looks like an imitation of Western patterns, but is more a question of entering into the inheritance of civilized man. The fact that the new African states have emerged in the period when many Western democracies were preoccupied with schemes of social welfare has contributed to their interest in the same field, but this is not in itself born simply of a desire to imitate.

The application in this context of the term 'middle class' to Asia and Africa can be misleading; that it is generally 'professional' in composition is axiomatic, as is the fact that most of its members have derived from groups that were already

7

marginally privileged to the extent that they had access to the beginnings of a full education. Where they have been politically triumphant it is because they have succeeded in conveying, genuinely or otherwise, the identity of their ultimate political and economic interests with those of the masses. In Africa, in terms of tribe or class origin, the new leaders tend to be more broadly based than in Asia and are conditioned by the fact of having come more quickly to the point of making uncompromising demands for independence. No examination of this phenomenon can omit to cite the case of the Convention People's Party in Ghana. It was born as a mass party with a branch in every village, and quickly became the state. Opposition, never more than an incoherent group of dissidents, was brushed aside. The Ghanaian elite, in the professional sense, are critical of the less well-educated politicians who lead it, but they have nevertheless played a leading role in its success by providing a relatively efficient administrative backing for its plans and policies. The dangers of a single elite acting without mass support are perhaps less where unity has been so imposed and moulded than in circumstances like those in Nigeria where loyalties are divided; it is significant that the trials in 1963 of Chiefs Awolowo and Enahoro, themselves members of the modern Yoruba elite, disturbed the mud of dissidence rather than, as must have been hoped by the Federal government, cleared the air. In Nigeria, the question is complicated by the fact that real power lies in different kinds of hands in different regions—in the north with the traditional rulers, in the west with the economically powerful cocoa farmers and their associates, and in the east with what can be regarded as a characteristically nationalist radical group. But all these elements and most of those elsewhere are affected by the will to appear modern.

The claim that the masses of Asia and Africa still embedded in their centuries old pattern of village life desire to be 'modern', to be in the main stream of world events, seems at times incongruous. The leadership elite often make it and, if they are right, it is some proof of their own effectiveness. Many African politicians, themselves 'modern' in outlook, are attacked, not for outraging tradition, but for being insufficiently dynamic. The Nigerian press has frequently been the vehicle for such a charge against its 'moderate' Prime Minister, Sir Abubakar Tafawa Balewa, and Mr Julius Nyerere, in resigning from the Premiership of Tanganyika in January 1962, was clearly showing his sensitivity to similar criticism and interpreting it in his own way as an incentive to restore his own full contact with the people and the TANU party machine. Competition over the degree of 'modernization' projected on the achievement of independence is one of the factors helping to provide a substitute for the desire to be free from colonial rule. It may be the source of a new form of extremism but since modernity is expensive this tends eventually to be limited by economic resources. Nevertheless, change is the keynote of new societies in the twentieth century. What does this entail? How does it affect the roles of the various national institutions?

In a social democracy the welfare of the people is the accepted motive force. The elites in new states assert their acceptance of this faith. Everything done is in the interests of the nation, whether it is the expulsion of the 'reactionaries' from government by a military junta, the acquisition of a prestige international airline or the construction of a hydroelectric scheme at vast expense. The desire to appear 'modern' in the eyes of the rest of the world is probably more compulsive than modernity for its own sake, but one has only to visit the better-known capitals of Africa to realize its significance for the development of the underdeveloped. It may, of course, lead to the verge of bankruptcy, but the incidental acquisitions are of paramount importance. The multiplication of university institutions rather than the expansion of one may not be the most economical method of procedure but it gives education an emphasis which is sometimes lacking, and it is certainly an expression of the articulate will of the people.

The same is true of the adoption by the elite of the cause of science and technology, and, because there is rarely the educational infrastructure to make expansion in this field possible on an indigenous basis, this makes for realistic co-operation with the advanced industrial societies which can make it practicable. This partly accounts for the niche which Israel has created for herself, in that she has the skills untainted by a colonial past; her only handicap is her situation *vis-à-vis* the Arab states, but, as

9

Pan-Africanism becomes more specifically Black African, so this diminishes in importance. Where the elite is very small and the knowledge of the technologies exceptionally limited, the officers of the armed forces assume a particular significance. They become, at least in their own eyes, the champions of modernity, the only group with the 'know-how' to run an advanced society. This accounts for the prominence in politics in the Middle East and parts of Asia of the military revolutionary. In sub-Saharan Africa the number of officers with any real technical experience behind them is as yet so small that this situation has not yet arisen.

The emphasis on technology has also tended to widen the development gap between the rural areas and the main urban centres. The political initiative, except in areas like Northern Nigeria, has shifted from the village to the town. Even in countries such as Tanganyika where the existing towns, even the capital, are small and widely scattered, this is largely true. The Ashanti farmers' distrust of the coast 'verandah boy' has become in ten years an almost universal phenomenon. It may be that the attraction of the city is proving more important than any other factor in achieving detribalization to the point where allegiances are transferred. In relation to the tribal composition of an army, and especially of an officer corps, the importance of this needs little emphasis.

At the same time as the city exercises its attraction and makes of the elite an essentially urban class at the centre of the nation's affairs, so some facets of a new administration disturb those who have had the closest connections with those foreign institutions which have gradually been 'purified' during a long period of gradual development. In former British territories, this applies particularly to the civil service and the army; the tendency to suspect the politicians and to be perturbed by their reputations is a significant factor in generating the political cohesion of the elites. Coincidentally, the capacity to speak for the masses is generally deteriorating on the part of both groups. In one case, wealth acquired by dubious means tends to enhance the gap, and in the other, rates of pay tailored for expatriates, with built-in inducements, and inherited by indigenous officers and officials are a cause of economic division. On occasions, the right to regular leave in Europe has been a point of controversy for Africans in such positions. A new society needs a wider dispersion of the economic benefits of 'progress' as well as of power and initiative; otherwise it is likely to fall prey to revolution or suffer from the instability which derives from disunion. The specific danger is the displacement of tribal and regional rivalries by new jealousies essentially economic in origin, but also rooted in differences of outlook.

The possibility of the elite's revulsion from the machinations of the politicians has already been mentioned. Its connection with the tendency to opposition, natural to those who enjoy the benefits of higher education, requires examination. Few army officers in African states, for example, have been university educated, but many of them have experienced what they regard, in terms of prestige, as the equivalent, at Sandhurst or St Cyr. Because they have been at institutions isolated in themselves from nationalist politics, this does not mean that they have no affinity with their civilian counterparts. They have regular contact with those at universities in the same countries with whom eventually they share the 'been-to' label which has something of the value to them of the Old School Tie. Back in their own countries the very smallness of the elite draws them into society with the products of local universities. There have been occasions when such universities have seemed to be the repositories of public opinion and the reflection of it. The angry reaction to the announcement of the Anglo-Nigerian agreement in 1960, fanned from dubious quarters though it was, is a case in point. The student demonstration and invasion of the Parliament building was improper and deplorable, but it commanded a large measure of public and parliamentary support. It is difficult to separate the sources of informed opinion in developing countries from the existing elite and its potential recruits. The reservoir, even in an enormous country like Nigeria, is inevitably small. This suggests the importance for national unity, in an indirect as well as a direct way, of the armed forces and other national institutions which are at once cohesive and drawn from different regions and levels of society, which are both providing vocational training and educating their personnel in a more general way.

The transference of loyalty over the period of independence

from the traditional organization to an institution expressive no longer of imperial rule but of national sentiment, is of value in a number of diverse ways. Though military and similar disciplines are generally supposed to involve a submergence of individuality in advanced societies, it may be that in different environments they have a liberating effect. Pride in appearance, in physical fitness, in one's own skills in particular directions, are essential constituents of an ethos of this sort. Inevitably they involve a weakening of the more primitive religious beliefs which take little account of individual dignity, and they instil a confidence which, while essential for national progress, can also be turned to revolutionary ends. At the same time, while the institution itself, because it gives reasonable pay and provides good conditions of service, breaks the bonds of poverty, the process of training is concerned with personal qualities and thus tends to create an atmosphere in which 'the rights' of the individual assume some meaning. A periodic return to the home environment may lead to re-assimilation but, if not too prolonged, is just as likely to stimulate comparisons of the kind which are the first signs of political and social consciousness. The recruitment of police, soldiers or workers in nationalized industries like the railways or dock and harbour boards, is almost always followed by intensive elementary education. The acquisition of a degree of literacy enhances the feelings mentioned, and places the individual into a new category in relation to his elders in the tribe or family. Inevitably he is in demand to read, and write, and begins to realize the extent to which his capacity for choice and advancement is obstructed by a system which no longer seems as rational as it did.

Given a society of this nature, the possibilities not only of driving a wedge between the political leaders and the masses, but of distinguishing between the officers and men in national forces are, therefore, seen to diminish. It does not require an exaggerated concern for 'the welfare of the men' on the part of the officer to establish some identity of interest between them. The view that men of one tribal group are not likely to respond to leadership from officers of another which they hold to be inferior may be of some significance in day-to-day military or police affairs, especially those involving danger or hardship, but it is not necessarily of any great importance when considering the question of reliability in the face of some political crisis. Where the armed forces are used deliberately to generate civic consciousness its validity is certainly in doubt.

The course of political development in a new state depends on many factors. The most recently independent non-Moslem countries are perhaps those most firmly addicted to the Western model in spite of the gestures of friendship to the Soviet bloc. They are more likely for this reason to resist oligarchic tendencies unless they feel that drastic action has been forced upon them. Unlike the European countries, they are not in the position of feeling their way to an unknown political goal. They have patterns in which they can discern the features most suitable to their own circumstances and condition. It is easy to take the examples of emergency repressive legislation, which are characteristic not only of new states but of unstable old ones, and draw the conclusion that the dictatorial one-party state is the aim which the new leaders have set themselves. This will especially seem to be the case to those members of the more sophisticated elites who find themselves in gaol for opposition activities. But cynicism about political motives can be carried too far. The criteria which are used in public speeches for the assessment of current issues by the Mboyas, Nyereres, Obotes and others are those of democratic practice and human rights and liberty. Respect for communist achievement is genuine and widespread, especially in Africa where technological attainment in the space race is much admired, but knowledge of the domestic arrangements of communist states is rudimentary and coloured by a similar idealism about Marxism to that which used to be fashionable amongst Western intellectuals.

When considering the place and role of the military in new societies, their insecurity and instability are first considerations. They are seeking a way stamped with their own individuality, and at the same time require an adequate machinery of authority in the traditional mould. The armies of Africa would be inadequate for this purpose were it not for the legacy of efficient police forces, at any rate in English-speaking territories. Like the civil service and the police, the military have to adjust to the problem of working with politicians, who may be of different political hues. The officers are inevitably more completely implicated in the development of national consciousness than are those in old established countries who can take it for granted. They are part of a small elite, they have close contacts amongst the civil servants and the politicians, they are well known to each other and many of them have enjoyed the same common but in a sense unique experience of training in a closed institution overseas. They are typical in some ways of the new men in their countries, but are at the same time the inheritors of an especial kind of foreign tradition which has come down through the agency of a foreign army and been consciously adapted to the conditions of a defence force under colonial administration.

II

New Armies—The Legacies of Imperial History

THE ADJUSTMENT OF MILITARY forces to the conditions
of independence is a slow process. For a number of
reasons, primarily the lack of educated manpower and the
fact that defence institutions are themselves an essential expression of imperialism, their adaptation to the fresh circumstances
has a low priority even in the minds of the politicians who must
rely on them. The armies of new states tend to retain their
colonial flavour, their foreign advisers and their affinity with
Europe longer than do the civilian public services. For this
reason the history and traditions of the defence forces out of
which they emerge is of exceptional importance.

A civil service can safely continue the appearance, the
forms and the performance of its pre-independence counterpart
without incurring odium. For though civilian officials may be
petty or corrupt, it has not been usual for them in the great
twentieth-century empires to be personally oppressive or vin-
dictive. They may have had to carry out unpopular policies and
even in certain instances may have made them worse by their
own maladministration, but ultimately they have not been
demonstrably responsible for the consequences. The police and
the army have had to clear up the disorder they may have left.
In such a way the military may have become associated with

unpleasant memories of the past, and a reputation for harshness is not easily lost, especially in societies which are not yet in the full flush of development. There is no need to look beyond Irish history to appreciate what such a legacy, when sustained by overlong historical memories, may mean. Thus in some areas of the world of new states today, the army stands for punitive expeditions and for policies otherwise largely forgotten, or for 'brutal and licentious soldiery' left at a loose end, as it were, after wars which the local people ill understood.

But it is not only the defence force as an instrument of domestic policy or its members behaving improperly in idle moments, which affect the standing of its modern successor. The new army may well have inherited a composition and a method of recruitment which is a liability after independence. Thus a policy designed to maintain the balance and effectiveness of a colonial army may have precisely the opposite effect in a newly freed state. A literate majority is likely to resent a force composed deliberately of illiterate minority groups from some remote corner of the territory. This may have been the best kind of force to show unquestioning allegiance to the expatriate officers, but it is not likely to respond or appeal to representatives of the local educated elite in the same way. Politically, an army composed of tribes with long established warrior tendencies may be a dangerous anachronism in a state in whose other institutions the so-called unwarlike peoples predominate. At a slightly more remote period in history—though in most of the countries under consideration the relevant time scale is not overlong—the embryonic armies have sometimes been composed almost entirely of slaves. This is a taint not calculated to make the best impression on the new elite, or even on the peasant farmer reasonably secure in the knowledge of his own independence. But such speculative generalizations have little validity; almost every particular case is *sui generis* and only a series of examples focused on particular aspects of local military history can adequately convey their importance to the modern successor armies. It is strange, and encouraging or pathetic according to the viewpoint, to contemplate the extent to which an adherence to custom appears at times to cut sharply across modern political inclinations, but it is doubtful whether the old regimental shibboleths, even though they may be retained, have much practical meaning in the new context.

India

In the space of such a survey a detailed discussion of the historical origins of the British Indian Army is not practicable. Its development out of the East India Company's regiments of the late eighteenth and early nineteenth century is comparatively well known. The expansion of British rule in India through the Punjab, Sind and up to the borders of Afghanistan, through the agency of troops who were essentially mercenaries and for the most part glad to be so, is part of the vague historical knowledge of many products of the English educational system. The event, if not the circumstances, of the Indian mutiny, is well understood but its lasting impact on the Indian army scarcely appreciated. It is fashionable now to take the view that Anglo-Indian race relations were already deteriorating when the Sepoys broke out in revolt. The accuracy of this claim can hardly be disputed, but its acceptance disguises the traumatic effect on the participants, and their descendants on either side, of the event itself. A few instances of the cautious awareness of danger which it instilled into the official mind dwelling on military problems adequately illustrate its true nature and implications for an independent Indian army nearly a century later.

Expressed briefly, the mutiny meant that the principle of racial equality, accepted just before its outbreak in the Civil Service, had no chances in the army. The fear that a force, which was homogeneous and coherent, would be a grave security risk was paramount. Nationalities and castes, religions and creeds all had to be mixed up indiscriminately. Sir Charles Wood, writing to Sir Hugh Rose on February 26, 1862, stated the case for making the army safe brutally and succinctly: 'I wish to have a different and rival spirit in different regiments, so that Sikh might fire into Hindu, Goorkha into either, without any scruple, in case of need.'[1] The class company regiments of the Punjab and Bengal were a device to provide a built-in rivalry, a system of

[1] The Wood Papers, X.50, quoted in Hira Lal Singh, *Problems and Policies of the British in India, 1885–98*, Asia Publishing House, London, New York and Bombay, 1963.

checks and balances against sedition within each battalion. An interesting beneficial by-product of religious segregation, which was justified to some extent by dietary differences, was the ease with which the army was distributed in 1947 between India and Pakistan even though in the meantime religious antagonism may have been encouraged.

The system of separation was in fact progressively extended, until, by 1890, in the Bengal army the majority were one-class regiments and, it is said, a better type of recruit was forthcoming. In this way, it was felt, the spread of subversion could best be prevented. The essentially mercenary nature of the old British Indian army and its isolation by these means from the main trend of national events has created its own problems for the post-independence force. The same was true of the recruitment policy adopted; apart from the long drawn out process of establishing Indian officers in their own right, which will be considered later, the method of raising other ranks underwent a number of changes with special implications. Hira Lal Singh in the book already quoted describes how, after the mutiny, the emphasis switched, naturally enough, from Oudh to Nepal, the Punjab and the North West Frontier. It was in this period that Gurkhas came to be regarded as the most reliable and the best soldiers. There were nevertheless dangers in concentrating too heavily on the so-called warlike classes and these were overcome by postings to areas remote from their homeland in the effort to confirm their allegiance to the Raj. Such manoeuvres were justified as a matter of imperial policing, but they scarcely laid the best foundations for the establishment of a free united India sure of its national destiny and of statehood. After independence, deliberate measures were required to enable the army to play a role as a national melting pot fusing diverse elements together in the fire of common service.

In view of the joint administration of Burma with India until 1937, it is not surprising that there were marked similarities in the military legacies to the two countries. The Arakan Light Infantry, which had been raised in 1824, was in fact disbanded after the Indian Mutiny. During the first world war there were four battalions of Burma Rifles each raised on a 'class company' basis, but after 1925 specifically Burmese recruitment was suspended and each battalion consisted of two companies of Karens, one of Kachins and one of Chins. The effect of the Indian tradition of 'warrior peoples' was, therefore, unfortunate; loyalties grew inevitably on a class and community basis rather than being identified with the nation. The expansion of the forces after 1937, moreover, saw the promotion of other races to the higher ranks and left the Burmese with a sense of resentment, which it is little exaggeration to say found vent in the Burma National Army during the Japanese occupation, in itself a source of instability in the independence period.

By way of contrast, in Malaya, where the approach to military institutions was, to say the least, cautious, recruitment was gradually extended from the Federated Malay States to every state and settlement and in the 1930s the army could be described as the only unifying influence throughout the whole country; but this was in a territory where the lack of political consciousness was marked almost to the point of unhealthiness.

Egypt

The Egyptian army has almost as long a history as that of India. The ancestor of the force we know today was raised by Mehemet Ali between 1805 and 1849. There had been a military mutiny against the Turkish governor and foreign advisers were called in to create a modern force. From Mehemet's time onwards, the Khedive maintained a considerable army but it was in no real sense identified with national development and consciousness until the rise of Nasser's generation of officers after 1938. Actually, in Egypt at large there was a deep suspicion of the military, derived from the fact that before the beginning of the nineteenth century the armed force in the country had been basically Turkish, providing little opportunity for native Egyptians.

It was in 1820 that Mehemet Ali took the decisive step of establishing an officers' school at Aswan in Upper Egypt. This was directed by Frenchmen, but there was still heavy reliance on Turkish and Albanian sources for officer material. A few Egyptian recruits were forthcoming in the 1820s, a General Staff and Command School was set up at Khanka in 1823, but in essence the officer corps remained foreign until the twentieth century. It is true that under Said's rule a small Egyptian nucleus was created, and that the Khedive Ismail between 1863 and 1879 established military schools and a staff college, but at this time the tendency was towards Europeanization. This created a measure of professionalism and *esprit de corps* which probably helped to exaggerate the consequences of the enforced retirement in 1879 of 2,500 officers for reasons of economy. This brought down the Nubar government and a chain reaction led to the deposition of Ismail. A new law for military service was passed in 1880 only to encounter the opposition of Arabi Pasha. This law included a four-year term of service with five subsequent years on the reserve, and it was Arabi's contention that it constituted a long-term hindrance to the establishment of an Egyptian officer corps. Four years' compulsory service in the ranks was unlikely to provide an adequate time for the individual to prepare for assumption of officer status. A series of demands were made against the government culminating in a revolt which to some extent represented the growth of Egyptian nationalism at large. There is some significance in the fact that Arabi came from a humble background: he was the son of a village headman and had not received much education.

The fact that after 1882 the Egyptian forces were essentially subordinate to the British establishment effectively removed them from the struggle for liberation from foreign domination, at any rate until the 1920s. The lead was taken by other professional groups. After 1922, when Egypt was declared an independent kingdom, political consciousness spread fairly rapidly throughout all sections of the community even though the Wafd party was entirely dominant. From 1945, however, the King, Farouk, increasingly overrode the Wafd politicians, and while retaining control over and the allegiance of the army's hierarchy, was unable to capture the loyalty of the younger elements amongst the officers. Thus the failure to establish an indigenous military tradition in Egypt over many decades eventually reaped its own reward—a revolution in which the young army professionals emerged as the political power.

In India, the British developed an army which, having been one of the strongest pillars of imperialism in the whole Indian Ocean area, was at the same time capable of conversion into a national army. What is more, it has proved to be a national army without, as yet, any aspirations to political control. It remained the loyal servant of the Nehru-Congress Party government in spite of the setback experienced in the clash with China in the latter part of 1962. Perhaps more completely than any other extra-European force it has inherited the apolitical tradition. Elsewhere, as in Egypt, armies which the British played a substantial role in establishing have taken the opposite turning, in this particular case because of the frustrations of the 'new men' in the officer corps closely associated with the nationalist political movement. The same explanation, however, does not hold good for the Sudan, where development had been akin to that in India with a slow but steady build-up, from 1918 onwards, of officers for the Sudan Defence Force educated at Gordon College, Khartoum, and the Sudan Military College and also for short periods at British military training schools. The army coup in November 1958 was apparently caused by a crescendo of impatience with the inefficiency and corruptibility of the politicians and owed a good deal to the example of Pakistan. In fact, these two cases, both in predominantly Moslem countries, illustrate the academic dangers of treating military development historically as separate from more general political trends. The fact that the armies of India on the one hand, and Pakistan and the Sudan on the other, given similar histories, have behaved differently after independence makes inferences more difficult to draw but does not invalidate the view that the history of an imperial force has a bearing on the development of the national army which succeeds it. The armies of Commonwealth West Africa have not yet crystallized into their indigenous form and, for them, therefore, the nature of the past's influence has still fully to reveal itself.

Commonwealth West Africa

The West African Frontier Force (WAFF) was founded by Lugard in 1898 in response to the threat of French encroachments. It had its origins in quasi-military constabulary and had seen service on an inter-territorial basis. Until the disbandment of Headquarters, West Africa Command, in 1956, just before Ghana's independence, the tendency to think of the area from the Gambia to Nigeria as a whole was an essential part of British imperial strategic thinking. Though a joint training school remained at Teshie, near Accra, until 1960, and even since then the Sierra Leone force has used Nigerian facilities at Kaduna, there is no particularly strong affinity remaining between the three forces of Ghana, Nigeria and Sierra Leone. Political developments have frustrated such a possibility, though common organizations, customs and equipment remain.

At an early stage in the development of colonial military institutions in West Africa, Nigerian troops of the Lagos Constabulary took part, under Captain John Glover, RN, in Wolseley's Ashanti Campaign of 1873–74. After its creation in 1886, the Royal Niger Company formed its own constabulary and it was a detachment of this force which played a useful role in the Bida and Ilorin expeditions of 1897. The Niger Coast Protectorate had its origin in the delta, and in fact was known for a time as 'the Oil Rivers Irregulars'. Its main duty was to protect commerce on the Niger. Similar developments took place in the Gold Coast. After the final Ashanti Campaign in 1900, the WAFF was consolidated, and absorbed most of the constabulary forces into its regiments. The Southern Nigeria Regiment, for instance, consisted of the Lagos and Niger Coast Constabularies and a proportion of the Royal Niger Company's force; the Gold Coast Constabulary became the Gold Coast Regiment; and a similar development took place in Sierra Leone. In assessing the significance of the imperial military legacy to Nigeria the prominent part played by WAFF regiments in the expeditions against Bida, Kontagora, Yola, Bornu, Zaria and, of course, Kano and Sokoto in the first five years of this century should not be overlooked. It is perhaps fortunate that the amalgamation of the two Nigerian protectorates and of the two regiments in 1914 was followed immediately by service outside Nigeria. Throughout British West Africa in the first and second world wars, the fact of common service and fresh experience overseas was of paramount importance not only in stimulating political consciousness amongst the soldiers but in encouraging memories of internal punitive expeditions to fade, even though, as far as Western Nigeria was concerned, these were dramatically revived by the Egba rising of 1918. The problems of Abeokuta are an interesting illustration of the way in which the military sometimes incur the odium which should be reserved for those responsible for the policy which led to riot and disorder.

Operations against the Germans in the Cameroons and Togoland in 1914–15 brought together WAFF units from the different territories in co-operation with French overseas troops, mainly Senegalese Tirailleurs. The effect of serving, there and in East Africa, against German-recruited African neighbours does not seem to have been in any way remarkable; there is little or no evidence of any reaction comparable to the sense of guilt experienced at a much later date when action against 'fellow Africans' was required of the United Nations forces in the Congo. Before the second world war, the force, now the RWAFF, was organized on the basis which prevailed until independence. Recruitment of other ranks was normally confined to the northern bush areas or hinterland of each territory. 'The right type of recruits' were the illiterates with a warrior tradition and preferably of the Moslem religion. The influence of the Indian experience is as clear in this field as it was when Lugard created Kaduna on the pattern of a South Asian military canton-ment. Until recently, there were still serving in the Nigerian and Ghana forces men from French-speaking areas of West Africa. They came from the remote areas of what are now Upper Volta and Niger, and especially from around Lake Chad. The recruitment of southerners from the coastal areas began when the demand for clerks, drivers and other minor technicians built up during the second world war. The contrast between the effect of the volunteer system in British West Africa and of conscription in the French territories can easily be exaggerated; in their different ways ex-servicemen throughout the territories from the Sahara to the Congo have played a prominent part in moulding the political development of their countries.

French West and Equatorial Africa

The conquest of millions of square kilometres of French Africa was achieved by African troops commanded by French officers. Chiefs were used as agents for the supply of men and even in the period before 1939 nationalists were crying out for the abolition of conscription and the restriction of volunteers to local service. Nevertheless, even though in later years the

Rassemblement Démocratique Africain (RDA) was to oppose the use of French West African troops in North Africa and at Suez, there was genuine loyalty to France in her hour of crisis in 1940.

Figures and examples of reaction in different territories to the problem of military service are significant. In the first world war about 180,000 French African troops served on the Western Front, and in Senegal the first African Deputy, Blaise Diagne, succeeded in securing concessions on citizenship rights as a *quid pro quo* for this remarkable contribution to the war effort.[1] Again in 1939, the right to vote for colonial councillors was extended to all those who had completed military service. In Dahomey in 1948, 58 per cent out of the 54,000 electorate were ex-servicemen or serving soldiers.[2] In various territories, however, problems arose which illustrate well the difficulties of establishing and maintaining a satisfactory image of the armed forces and may still be a factor in uneducated memories. For instance, in 1912 on the Ivory Coast, military recruitment, even though there were abundant volunteers, became confused in some people's minds with the sale of the best human specimens into slavery not so many years before—an understandable reaction to the rigours of recruit training. At one stage some of the inhabitants of the Assini area actually fled across the frontier into the Gold Coast to avoid their obligations.

Between the wars, in French West Africa alone about 10,000 men were recruited annually, with the well-recognized effects on agricultural areas when a high proportion of able-bodied males are withdrawn from the business of providing for survival. Accelerated recruitment in the war period was not followed by an added awareness of the subsequent problem of demobilization. Thompson and Adloff, in their book already quoted, have commented on the difference in treatment meted out to French overseas and French metropolitan veterans. The devoted loyalty of men imbued with martial traditions to their French officers, whom they tended to equate with chiefs, was not rewarded by an adequate system of compensation and pensions. In 1948, a mission was sent out under Commandant

[1] Virginia Thompson and Richard Adloff, *French West Africa*, George Allen & Unwin, London, 1958, p. 109.
[2] *Ibid.*, p. 58.

Henri Ligier to investigate the grievances which were coming to a head. Even in the 'fifties the problem lingered on and, though jobs were reserved for veterans, conscription was undoubtedly responsible for the migration of some of the population to British territories. However, when the French recognized that their possessions in Africa ought to be integrated into the Western defence system, conditions were improved and a more than tentative Africanization of the officer corps was initiated.

Though at first there was less cause to raise African troops in Equatorial than in West Africa and, in any case, Senegalese soldiers were drafted in from time to time, the history of Afrique Equatoriale Française (AEF) has also been influenced by the problems of the colonial forces. Compulsory service was introduced in 1919, and in 1942 there were about 10,000 men from AEF serving in General Leclerc's Free French Army. After the war, it was necessary to establish the principle of equality between the pay of French and overseas soldiers before an adequate number of recruits was forthcoming from the Sara country. By this time, however, there was a formidable organization of 15,000 veterans who intended to dominate the local administration in Chad and what is now the Central African Republic. Semi-military villages were established in the Logone region, residence in which required a qualification of fifteen years' military service. The impact of the military varied inevitably from area to area; in Chad the long early period of military administration may be said to have inhibited political development, while in Gabon ex-soldiers soon emerged as part of the growing new elite.

These examples of the variations in the history of and official attitude to the colonial armies in Asia and Africa serve largely to illustrate the difficulty of generalizing about the military legacy. Nevertheless, when patterns of recruitment and the establishment of indigenous officer corps are considered, common factors are readily perceived; more important, however, is the behaviour of the armies during the colonial period, for it is often this which is today responsible for a tarnished image. Popular attitudes may still be conditioned by incidents,real or legendary, which occurred in an earlier phase of political development.

25

III

Armies and the Achievement of full Independence—Egypt and Latin America

I N NO CASE IN recent times has the contribution of a
military elite to the achievement of final independence from
foreign domination been more clear cut than in Egypt. This,
as already suggested, is directly connected with the history of
Egypt's armed forces over the last century and a half. To under-
stand the events of the last twelve years there is no need to go
back further than 1882 when Britain effectively occupied Egypt
after the Arabi Pasha rebellion, for towards the end of that year
the new overlords virtually disbanded the Egyptian army as such.
They established in its place a new force of their own creation
under a British commander. The local system by which a cash
payment could secure exemption from military service was not
discouraged and the result was a force consisting of those who
were unable to pay the price.

After 1918, there was a long struggle between the rising
nationalist influences and the British for control of the force.
The retention of a foreign inspector-general was the principal
bone of contention and even after the relative independence
achieved as a result of the Anglo-Egyptian Treaty of 1936,
Egypt was bound by its term to rely on British sources for the
supply of equipment and a cadre of instructors, technical and
otherwise. The key event however, did take place in that year

when the Wafd government opened the doors of the military academy in such a way as to allow true Egyptians, of whatever origin and social and economic standing, to seek commissions. The effect was immediate, for there graduated from the Academy two years later the majority of those who were to constitute the Free Officers' Group and lead the revolution, notably the future Colonel Nasser himself.

Subsequent experience, especially disgust at the incompetent conduct of the Arab-Israeli war in 1948, bound them together. Most of them had enjoyed a secondary school education, taken part in student agitation in the 1930s and felt the frustrations consequent upon British dominance in their country during the 1939–45 war. They were thus typical of the new elite in such countries and may be said to have much in common with their opposite numbers in the colonial territories proper.

The characteristic feature of Egyptian social development was, and probably remains, an overproduction of educated men in relation to the opportunities available to them in society. The military element in the elite found their own outlet in 1952, and it still remains to be seen to what extent they can satisfy the aspirations of others.

Egypt, of course, was never a colony, but though the limits of British authority were ill defined the European community enjoyed a privileged commercial and legal, as well as social position. Plans for social reform were only slowly put into effect. Though free elementary education was agreed upon in 1925, only about two-thirds of the relevant age group were enjoying its benefits by 1960. There was, however, a disproportionate development of university education resulting in a large group still in their twenties who have yet to come to terms with the military elite. It was not until after the 1952 coup that a course on 'Arab Society', the equivalent of a civics course in an English school, was introduced as a compulsory feature of secondary and higher education. Earlier graduates of the Egyptian system received little formal instruction in the political and social issues of the day. The military regime has done its best to compensate for this, though inevitably nationalist propaganda is a prominent feature of this section of the curriculum. There is, however, no more doubt about the source of the impetus to educational development than about that of economic progress in modern Egypt.

The committee which founded the so-called Free Officers' Group in 1949 consisted of eleven men, eight of whom had graduated from the Military Academy in 1938, two in 1939 and one in 1940.[1] They came not from the traditional aristocratic background of those of Turkish or Albanian descent, but from pure Egyptian stock. Nasser himself appears to have taken a full part in the political agitation leading to the establishment of the Wafd government in 1936. His subsequent development and that of most of his colleagues was affected by incidents like the pressure applied to King Farouk to recall Nahas Pasha in February 1942; the fact that this was achieved by a ring of British tanks round the Abdin Palace was more important to them than the nature of the ensuing political change. This does not mean, however, that the Free Officers' movement was compounded of rash revolutionaries without a programme. The reverse was the case; Nasser had a clear philosophy (expressed in his *The Philosophy of the Revolution*) which derived from an awareness of the social and economic problems of Egypt. He got his chance to spread ideas on these subjects when in 1951 he became an instructor at the Army Staff College. Thus a movement which until 1949 had entirely lacked cohesion now acquired a spearhead. The failure of the monarchy to hold its own with Britain drew to it the hostility of the new men.

Like almost all such politico-military groups, the Free Officers' organization had originated on a personal and individual basis. They simply shared a common training experience, an *esprit de corps* derived from it, and a sense of frustration. It is unlikely that many or any of them had deliberately joined the army for political ends. Their motives were probably not dissimilar from those prevailing amongst entrants to the officer corps in Commonwealth Africa today; the army is a career offering security, status, a high standard of accommodation and the opportunity for further education which becomes attractive as soon as entry to the more obvious civil occupations ceases to be easy. The immediate cause of the Group's coagulation was direct interference by the royal

[1] P. J. Vatikiotis, *The Egyptian Army in Politics: Pattern for New Nations?* Indiana University Press, Bloomington, 1961, pp. 45 *et seq.*

palace in the affairs of the army and in particular in senior appointments which were likely to have repercussions on the career opportunities of the younger men.

Once formed, however, the Free Officers' Group, steeped in the humiliating experience of the Arab-Israeli war, rapidly came to the point where it identified national freedom with the overthrow of the existing political regime, more especially the monarchy. Apart from seeking always to place their members in strategic positions throughout the army, they managed to establish close contacts with elements in the press. It is now a well-known fact that they organized a series of cells throughout large sections of the army. The now famous election to the committee of the Officers' Club in which for the first time the candidature of the Chief of Staff as the King's candidate was challenged, brought matters to a head. Success strengthened the Free Officers; and they avoided the obvious trap of being diverted into terrorist activities against the British Forces in the Canal Zone. This was followed by Farouk's attempt to appoint as Minister of War, his sister Fawzia's husband, a man without military experience.

A general state of political indecision in July 1952 presented the Free Officers' Group with the opportunity they wanted. They were able to appear as the champions of popular discontent, but they still required considerable luck, in the shape of incompetence on the part of their opponents, to succeed. The temporary placing of Neguib as a figurehead in a position of power was a necessary interim measure to consolidate the position of the army's new men as the champions of nationalist Egypt.

Up to this point it could be argued that this was a typical military revolution, but the fact is that within two years, an underground group had firmly established themselves as in most respects the leaders of the nation. Their debt to the military past was slight, except in so far as it created their opportunity to respond to the challenge of corrupt conservatism. The secret lies partly in the actual nature of the leadership. It was not that they were 'the intellectuals' for most of them had had technical, vocational and practical, rather than academic education. They had lived to themselves in a way which is not true of officer corps in the newer of the new states. They were assisted, therefore, in entrenching themselves by an assiduous campaign, the exact origin of which is hard to trace, aimed at suggesting that the army only intervened reluctantly when it was clear that other groups were unable to do so. The real intellectuals have been persuaded to think of their own deficiencies as responsible for the present situation: the ambitions of the officers are a secondary consideration. A sense of failure on the part of those with an academic education is, in fact, a quite logical reaction to the success of the military junta. The fact is that the intellectuals lacked unity and a sense of purpose. They have proved to be individual and collective failures. Those who might have been in this category find their imaginative capacity restricted by the Nasser regime, of which perhaps the most important characteristic is its determination to mobilize the economic resources of the nation without stimulating the kind of awareness of internal problems which might regenerate revolution.

In its early phases, the revolutionary group acted so quickly that opposition had no time to crystallize. They had to counter the influence of the Wafd, and more especially of the Muslim Brethren. They were aided by the traditional disposition of Egyptians to accept autocratic authority. As the time went on they were able to abandon the dubious methods by which individuals were isolated or removed from the political scene, and to use developments in the international field to enhance their prestige. The purchase of communist arms and equipment, opposition to the Baghdad Pact and ultimately the Suez crisis served to complete the domination of the army regime. Defiance of great powers is an important step in the assertion of national independence. The fact that the Anglo-French ultimatum in November 1956 preserved the Egyptian army from the full effects of what was on its way to being a second humiliating defeat by Israel was an important factor in the consolidation of the regime.

It is no accident that the army has emerged predominant in the Egyptian political scene and has become the symbol of national unity. Arab states are not by their nature cohesive; Islamic institutions are liable to command allegiance in a way which tends to prevent the easy development of overriding patriotic sentiment. The fact that, in any state, the army is the final repository of force without which the government's authority at home and abroad cannot be exercised is liable to assume, in certain circumstances, a vital importance. More significant in Afro-Asian new states, however, is the channel through which Western ideas, technical and political, reach the body of the state. In the case of Egypt, this was the army. It was not that it became a reservoir of engineering graduates, the only men with the 'know-how' to modernize in the whole community; it was simply that British and other European concepts of discipline and administrative efficiency permeated its younger elements. The Staff College training of a number of the Free Officers' Group was more important than might be supposed, for an apparently efficient administration on Western lines is one of the signs of progress most sought after in new states.

This particular example of an officer corps showing the way to national independence throws some light on the apparent irony of the apolitical British military tradition leaving behind it officers prone to become politicians. In Egypt, Nasser's group came to power partly because their views on the creation of an effective army had been disregarded while the validity of their arguments had been subsequently proved to all the world in Palestine in 1948. Thus, in Egypt, a new generation of officers concerned with military neatness and efficiency not only took over the reins of power but achieved for the first time full national independence.

The twenty states of Latin America have been subject to waves of militarism for a century and a half. Though it is possible to discern signs that this influence on politics is diminishing, the last thirty years have, in fact, been a period of exceptional activity in this respect. The military revolution in South and Central America has become a joke because of its frequency and its consequent temporary nature; to the outside observer it lacks the sense of purpose of, for instance, Nasser's regime in Egypt. There is, however, one basic similarity between the group of Latin-American states and the single Middle Eastern country: in both cases the army is politically prominent because of the contribution which it made to the achievement of independence; but, of course, the time scale is different and the Latin-American military have undergone many changes in the course of one hundred and fifty years.

Between 1945 and 1960, only four[1] of the Latin-American republics escaped military intervention in politics; but this does not mean that there is a close similarity between the military establishments in all the different states. The defence forces have proved fissiparous, fighting against each other and within themselves, and often being the victims as well as the instruments of individual and group ambitions. The process of achieving independence in Latin America was long drawn out and it seemed to make the use of force politically natural. The armies which helped to crystallize what was taken for freedom were not as a rule regular, professional forces; they were irregular organizations raised and employed to resolve obstinate political difficulties. If their action was successful—that is, if it succeeded in carrying with it, however temporarily, the mass of the people— then it was assumed to have acted in the interests of democracy. It was for this reason that representative institutions often survived in Latin America as a *façade*, but in practice revolutions were more important than elections and had virtually taken their place. It is popularly supposed that this addiction to military force was a direct inheritance from Spanish colonial rule, but, in spite of the nature of the original conquests of, for example, Peru and Mexico, the administration of the empire had been essentially civilian. On the other hand, like the North American pioneer, his Spanish counterpart further south was used to maintaining law and order with his own hands on the imperial frontiers and, therefore, used to violence.

In the early stages of the struggle for independence the identification between the military leaders and the political idealists was virtually total. But the length of the struggle blurred the issues; it was like the Wars of the Roses in England, in that violence became endemic and habitual. It needed the re-emergence of great leaders to give the people a concept of their own destiny and these were rarely forthcoming; as the years went by the chances of stability became less, often for economic reasons. A whole series of Henry VIIs able to reduce the warring groups to size would have been necessary. The seemingly inevitable result

[1] Uruguay, Costa Rica, Chile and Mexico. See *The Role of the Military in Underdeveloped Countries*, Ed. John J. Johnson, Princeton University Press, Princeton, 1962, p. 21.

was a growing gap between the military liberators and the people, to the point where the former acquired a vested interest in the central establishment of the state which they had created, and were prepared to abandon the idealists and support oppressive oligarchies often based on the landowning interest. But whether the groups actually achieving power were the privileged or regional gang-leaders, the military were ineffective in controlling them, and, even when they had the chance, did not attempt any fundamental change in the socio-economic systems which were at the root of the instability.

In the subsequent period up to the first world war, the Latin-American republics derived benefit from the industrial revolution taking place elsewhere. The improvement in transportation helped to mobilize their ability to provide resources of food and was amongst the factors which brought about an agricultural revolution in South America, which in its turn affected the structure of society. At the same time the extension of commerce in the cities attracted large volumes of population, and wealth became more widely spread than in the past. There was a corresponding development of nationalist feeling and political leaders began to think in similar terms to those employed by their opposite numbers in the nation states of Europe. Frontier clashes and expansionist policies led to demands for increases in the armed forces and even to a certain extent to local arms races. Missions from established European armies, especially that of Germany, were brought in to instil a professional outlook, and in a number of cases it was through the officer corps that countries were first introduced to the mysteries of science and engineering technology. Thus, for the second time in Latin-American history, the officers were in the revolutionary van, but in a number of states they were now drawn substantially from different groups within society; they were not aristocratic in origin to the extent which had previously prevailed, nor were the lower middle class able to compete any longer with the better educated young men from professional class stock who were attracted by the educational and social opportunities which the armed forces now seemed to provide. In one or two of the more advanced countries like Argentina and Chile these seemed sufficient to establish over a number of generations civilian rule supported by apolitical armies. The most important factor in establishing what looked plausibly like permanent stability was the fact that the private army could no longer compete against the expensive paraphernalia of the professional state force. In this way as in others the expert officer with technical training became essential to the developing nation, but at the same time the seed was sown of future dissent; the traditionalist was playing a part in development of a kind which sooner or later would bring about a revolution of its own in the industrialized cities. This process, linked with the rise of economic nationalism, eventually brought about the wave of military revolution which has taken place since 1936, and especially between 1945 and 1957.

The position of the military elite in Latin-American countries is due primarily to the role it has played at different stages in the struggle for independence. The composition of the leadership has generally changed in such a way as to match the needs of each individual country. Whereas once the Spanish and Portuguese rulers had been forced to withdraw in the early nineteenth century, the armed forces generally supported the privileged groups which took their place; in the first half of the twentieth century there has been a growing identification between the military and the urban masses. The conservatism of older generations of officers has, therefore, been replaced by the reforming enthusiasm of cliques of young officers. It is at this point that parallels with modern Egypt can more clearly be seen. The new men had lost patience with the landed and religious oligarchies and were, therefore, no longer necessarily prepared to support the traditional social order. The growth of strong navies and air forces introduced a new factor into the situation, especially as the armed forces as a whole were by no means fully occupied with military duties. But the new leaders did not, as the old had done, seek to impose policies; they tried to reflect popular movements even though this not infrequently led them into authoritarian postures and the elimination of opposition by denouncing all critics as 'enemies of the people'. In the end, however, such regimes have generally led to extreme left-wing activity which has produced its own reaction amongst the military leadership; the whole situation has been complicated by the usual personal rivalries and grievances about pay and promotion. The causes of military revolutions in twentieth-century Latin America have been many, but there has, in spite of appearances, been a tendency away from the Ruritanian type of petty palace conspiracy towards that deriving from deep social causes. At the same time, popular civil revolutions stood a decreasing chance of success without the aid of a section of the armed forces; this was, of course, due to the increasingly effective armament of the defence services and the police.

No mention has been made so far of the reactions of the other ranks of the forces to the changing social mood and their attitude towards the different phases of independence. Pay and perquisites, in countries with extremes of poverty, combined with a determination by commanders to achieve them, have been in most cases sufficient to isolate the soldiers and sailors from the people. Like the defence forces raised by colonial regimes, the men were often illiterate and, therefore, inclined to political apathy. Detestation of the military by the civil population, where it arose, rarely discriminated between officers and men. Such mutinies, or other rank risings as have taken place in Latin America in the twentieth century have been linked with grievances arising from economic depression; for instance, at the depth of the world slump in 1931, a battalion of the Peruvian army made an unsuccessful attempt at a *coup d'état* and in the following year sailors of the Ecuadorian navy mutinied. Only in Cuba[1] was an army revolution of this sort successful. By August 1933, the officer corps, even those who were not happy with the existing Machado government, had lost control of the situation and in the following month they were overthrown and replaced by their own men under the leadership of Sergeant Batista. This had the effect, not of breaking the army's influence in Cuban politics but simply of transferring it to new hands. Batista modernized the army and increased its size. Though he subsequently civilianized the administration and later surprisingly retired, he eventually returned to the Cuban scene in 1952 by organizing the young officers against the existing military hierarchy. Castro's revolution in its turn did, however, break the power of the professional army by achieving a military victory over regulars by irregulars.

[1] Edwin Lieuwen, *Arms and Politics in Latin America*, Frederick A. Praeger, New York, Revised Edition, 1961, pp. 97–100.

Thus in the last century and a half of Latin-American history the role of the military has undergone a number of changes. At times, only power for its own sake has interested the soldier, but at other times he has been the agent of nationalism. The military came into existence as a power group when the armies were allowed to outlive the wars of independence and at the same time retained some of the glamour of liberation. They then became the prey of disruptive and competing influences until such time as technological progress bequeathed to them the first real elements of professionalism. A straight comparison between the role of the military in Latin America over the whole period and that which is now evident in South-east Asia or the Middle East is impossible, for the simple reason that a kaleidoscopic development in twenty different countries has few permanent features. In a sense, the Latin-American experience has had something in common with that of all the other regions of the world at different times; phases in her past which correspond with the present in other countries may be discerned. Between them, her varied republics provide examples of virtually every possible relationship between the army and the civil element in a new state; but it would be fallacious to suppose that they provide a sound guide to modern trends elsewhere. The social structures of South and Central America, with the residual effects of centuries of both free and forced immigration still apparent, are not globally typical and, in any case, militarism, as a general phenomenon there, may well be in the final phase of its existence.[1]

[1] A comparison of the *current* political behaviour of armies by regions is attempted in Chapter XI.

IV

The Military Functions of Armed
Forces in New States

THE QUESTION AS TO whether a new state needs an army
of its own generally receives the same affirmative answer.
The reasons for this, on the whole, remarkable unanimity
are, however, not by any means entirely military. Given a
reasonable realism on the part of politicians, it would be strange
if they were. In the conditions created by the development of
modern weapons, few countries except the greatest of great
powers have any reasonable chance of defending themselves
against major aggression, and even those at the top of the pyramid
of power are prone these days to think in terms of interdependence. Judged by the relatively elementary criteria of frontier
defence, internal security and perhaps the possibility of partici-
pating in military adventures, the need of new states to possess
defence forces is, on the surface, doubtful; the implications of a
frank admission that they are an unjustifiable expense have,
nevertheless, in almost all recent cases proved a decisive deterrent
to disbanding them.

For large countries like India which have quite consciously
accepted at the time of independence a certain transfer of
responsibility for security in their own geographical regions,
there has been no real choice. In India's case, recent Chinese
actions are as complete a justification as any country could need

37

for the maintenance of substantial modern defence forces. There are not many other such clear-cut examples; Kenya leaders' reactions in this respect to the Somali claims to their Northern Frontier Province are scarcely parallel to the Indians' attitude to the disputes over the frontier in Ladakh and the meaning of the MacMahon line. Nor is this simply a question of scale even though the intensity of political feelings in the two cases might be equated. Though submission to the claims of Somali nationalism might incidentally be a first step towards the disintegration of the Kenyan state, Kenya is neither the fulcrum of a whole strategic area nor the victim of aggression by a great imperial power.

In the domestic field, as contrasted with that of external relations, it is easy for those resident in societies with a long record of stability to forget the part played by efficient security forces in making possible effective government. In states where the emphasis today is on the welfare and social security of the subject, the fact that law and order are fundamental prerequisites, tends to be obscured. Sophisticated societies have advanced a long way from Thomas Hobbes's concept that the duty of the sovereign is to provide 'law and order with some contentments'; 'the condition of man' in such communities is no longer in any ordinary sense 'a condition of war of everyone against everyone'. But one has only to read a so comparatively naïve account of the situation in the Congo as Richard Lawson's *Strange Soldiering*[1] to appreciate how easily in such an area 'the life of man' can become 'solitary, poor, nasty, brutish and short'.

Britain needed the administrative machinery for maintaining peace and enforcing the law not only, in the first instance, to weld divergent elements into one community but, later, to allow that measure of political and religious toleration which enables democracy to develop. New states in Africa and Asia, within whose often arbitrarily determined boundaries new nations are in the process of growth, are therefore confronted with problems encountered in parts of Europe in the seventeenth and eighteenth centuries or earlier, but in their attempts to solve them they are liable to be judged internationally by the criteria of the twentieth.

The withdrawal of the great imperial powers and the consequent transfer of power to fresh and often inexperienced hands,

[1] Hodder and Stoughton, London, 1963.

have indisputably increased the tendency to instability in some parts of the world. Administrative unity within artificial lines of demarcation may have made possible the emergence of relatively large political units where they were, half a century or less ago, only collections of loosely associated peoples, but it has not guaranteed their integrity. The breakdown of internal order may occur because of new-born political rivalries, but a more likely cause is traditional antagonism between ethnic and linguistic groups. It can, moreover, also arise where newly independent states fight amongst themselves in the pursuance of territorial claims or even to provide a distraction from severe internal crises. The danger of intervention in any of these circumstances by external forces anxious to exploit and create chaos for their own purposes is not negligible in the present state of East-West relations, though distance from the sources of power tends to diminish it. These are factors, not conclusive in themselves, which, perhaps fortunately for the peace of the world, cause the leaders of new states to pause and think before taking the brave decision to dispense with the military arm altogether.

Some of the shrewdest new leaders, notable for their concern for the welfare of the masses, have considered and been prepared to discuss openly the pros and cons of military nakedness. Amongst these have been Mr Julius Nyerere, the President of Tanganyika, and Dr John Karefa Smart, when responsible for defence in Sierra Leone. Both of these two men, and they were not alone, were from countries financially and economically weak, in which heavy expenditure on defence would quickly inhibit the limited capacity for development, they had also inherited exceptionally small forces from the British period— one and a half battalions in the first case and one battalion only in the second—which might therefore be supposed to serve little purpose. They had at their disposal recently expanded police forces which were normally adequate for the maintenance of order, because they had, and have, a limited military mobile capability. In the case of Tanganyika, however, the country was generally peaceful with frontiers which, although long, posed little threat, while Sierra Leone's diamond field and the adjoining international boundaries were a notorious source of violent unrest. The decision to retain a separate military force was common to both; in Sierra Leone any shrinkage in the reservoir of force seemed imprudent, in Tanganyika apart from prestige reasons, it was proper to think ahead to the needs of an incipient East African Federation.

Amongst the so-called Brazzaville group of states, the countries of the *Communauté française*, there has so far been no great enthusiasm for incurring the heavy financial burdens implicit in developing full-scale conventional armed forces. The presence, under a series of agreements the details of which have in no case been fully revealed, of French overseas troops obviously conveys a sense of security. The fact that at the time of President Fulbert Youlou's overthrow in August 1963, there were about 3,000 French troops in the vicinity of the capital of the Republic of the Congo at Brazzaville, suggests a military dependence on the former overlord not entirely consonant even with internal freedom of action. A speech made by President Houphouët-Boigny before the National Assembly of the Ivory Coast in January 1962 is representative of the official view in a number of the smaller Francophone states:

> It is important (he said) to remember that France no longer has any strategic interests in Abidjan; the French troops are stationed here at our request; there can be no doubt that France will be greatly relieved when she is asked to withdraw her troops.
>
> In the meanwhile, France provides our security until we can organize our own defence without indulging in heavy expenditure which will impede or wreck our economic development . . . but never shall an Ivory Coast soldier engage in an offensive action against an African state, and never shall our territory be used as an offensive base against an African country.

This, however, is an exceptional attitude not widely shared by states brought up in other traditions. The conventional view is that an army is a part of the essential paraphernalia of a new state, one without which independence will not be seen to have been completely achieved. It is thus a symbol of national prestige and of the apparent need to assert a community's standing in the eyes of the world. At its lowest level an inability to provide a guard of honour and a demonstration of military might for the benefit of a visiting Head of State would be regarded as in a sense diminishing national stature. The army joins the flag, the national anthem and other symbols, and in some cases is itself joined by national air and shipping lines, as the outward signs of independence and progress. It would be a blow too to national pride not to be able to make a contribution, however small, to a United Nations force such as that disposed in the Congo. In Africa, the desire to participate in the Congo operation has played a significant role in influencing the retention of inherited armed forces, and may even have been decisive in the case of Sierra Leone. Discussions, such as those amongst the Casablanca powers about the formation of the abortive Joint African High Command, are a powerful stimulant to the expansion of the armed forces of subscribing countries; it is not yet possible fully to gauge the parallel effects of the political and presumably eventually military campaign against South Africa which took form at the African Summit Conference at Addis Ababa in May 1963.

Such considerations as these are serving to complicate what began as an essentially simple pattern. Until they arose, it was an almost universal probability that in successor states the armed forces would continue to perform after independence the functions and duties previously established. In most cases, such forces, are, to begin with, simply colonial armies under another name; only a major change of foreign policy and, therefore, of military commitments could effect a drastic change in their basic tasks. In theory, apart from being released from any specific treaty commitments deriving from the policy of the imperial power, the continuance of which might destroy the desired image of neutralism, their responsibilities remain the same. In practice, neutralism and non-alignment involve a fundamental transformation of attitudes which, when combined with Pan-African and Afro-Asian aspirations, effectively change the whole scene. Within the Commonwealth, but to a lesser extent than in the *Communauté française*, this process is obscured by the retention of common organization, staff procedure, training methods, equipment and general attitude to military matters.

The main tasks of any army which is neither purely ceremonial nor created deliberately for an aggressive purpose are internal security and frontier defence, but the new trends towards internationalism running concurrently with the tide of nationalism have added new purposes. Kofi Baako, the Ghana

41

Minister of Defence, in a speech to the Accra Press Club on June 20, 1963, after referring to the social role of the armed forces (see Chapter V), enumerated their commitments as being to defend the territorial integrity of Ghana, to support the police in internal security, to contribute towards the defence of Africa and to contribute towards United Nations operations. This amounts to a typical expression of the African, if not necessarily the Asian, outlook in these matters.

Internal peace and resistance to external pressures may be most difficult to sustain in the hazardous period immediately following upon independence. The extent of reliance on the police in the first stages of any disorder varies according to the local tradition; in former British territories the policy is generally to use the army as a last resort, but in most of them there are strong mobile detachments of police which in every respect, including discipline and training in the use of small arms, are equivalent to an infantry striking force. The use of the army to provide the massive shock which is necessary to restore order has rarely been necessary in countries like Ghana or Nigeria, whether before or after independence. There is perhaps some significance in the fact that during the life of the Federation of Rhodesia and Nyasaland, when it was presumably developing towards the status of a new independent state—as in Southern Rhodesia—the distinction between the two types of security forces was not altogether maintained. In times of tension the army was sometimes—October 1960 for example—used to relieve the police of normal patrol duties. This can be said to incur the disadvantage that the army becomes too familiar to the ordinary citizen and, therefore, to some extent loses the advantage which it normally has over the police due to the possibility of removing it to a distance after sharp action has taken place and thus allowing time for the inevitable resentment to subside. The existence of a local gendarmerie force or any body habitually armed tends to blur and merge the images of the various forces in the public mind.

It is in internal security actions that the ethnic, tribal and religious composition of a force assumes its greatest importance. There are complex questions of morale and of the effectiveness of locally raised contingents against their own people. The Indian experience and practice, in spite of the policies described in Chapter II—or perhaps because the rules for their application were so carefully worked out—on the whole successfully prevented the army from inflaming religious antagonism and has had a profound influence in other Commonwealth territories. Lately in the final phases of colonialism there has been a deep awareness of the dangers of deliberately fomenting inter-tribal enmity for reasons of immediate expediency. The situation in Kenya would almost certainly be worse than it is if the Masai and other tribes had been worked up during the Mau Mau emergency into frenzied hatred of the Kikuyu. The difficulty is to strike the delicate balance between fraternization on the grounds of kinship between the security forces and the populace on the one hand, and the unnecessary violence which can result from the employment of virtually 'foreign' mercenaries, with no motive other than to loot and kill, on the other. The ultimate refinement of difficulty on the religious side was perhaps that in South Vietnam during the anti-Buddhist regime of President Ngo Dinh Diem when the army consisted of seventy per cent Buddhists, but nevertheless included homogeneous Roman Catholic units.

Frontier responsibilities are often linked with the internal situation, particularly where there is what has been fittingly described as 'tribal overspill'. The Somali problem in the Horn of Africa as it affects Kenya is the best example; the Ewe question as between Ghana and the Togo Republic is another such on a smaller scale. The majority of new states have for this reason or another at least one uneasy frontier; Burma and the Indo-China successor states spring readily to mind. In the latter area there has been internecine warfare between the states as communist influence has tried to force its way southwards to Saigon. The longer the frontier the greater the premium on mobility by mechanical means and the greater the strain on the resources of technically educated men. This in its turn may increase the reliance on foreign advisers which new states find to be almost inevitable in spite of the technical difficulties to which it can easily lead. There is no more striking example of this than South Vietnam, where the military coup in November 1963 revealed the even graver inherent dangers of a frontier and infiltration problem, and where the ruling group is pursuing a line of its own

43

without popular support. The restoration of military unity after the coup was made all the more difficult by the fact that those of North Vietnamese origin in the forces had been played off against South Vietnamese, that French trained officers were at loggerheads with those trained by the Americans, and, more seriously, that the Roman Catholic military minority was in violent opposition to the Buddhist majority.

Local conditions inevitably determine the nature, organization and equipment of national armies in new states; an interesting example of this was the almost complete abandonment of artillery as an operational arm in Commonwealth West Africa. Experience derived from the jungle warfare employment of mortars with the West African divisions in the Arakan during the last war had something to do with this, and it was in almost every respect a reasonable decision in the light of the most probable frontiers to be manned—the eastern boundaries of Nigeria and Ghana for instance—though not so sound in the event of the unlikely need to defend the north in either case.

The net effect of such specific assessments is to make the resulting units less than ideally suited to perform the functions of an expeditionary force. To undertake an external military adventure, or to contribute to a force aimed at releasing 'alien' hold on parts of Southern Africa, would involve the acquisition of an extensive range of equipment and experience which new states will not as a matter of course possess. Transport aircraft, airborne units and sound communications equipment are probably the first requirements, and at present only available in limited quantities. The United Nations intervention in the Congo has helped some young armies in respect of radio equipment but at the same time has exposed the essential weaknesses of individual countries and, in particular, the present reliance on the great powers for airlift. Talk of direct operations against the relics of colonialism, therefore, needs especially careful examination; it is unlikely that it would be undertaken, or, if it were, that it would have the remotest chance of real success unless it were to be supported by one or more of the major powers with ready access to the area. The particular case of 'the liberation' of South Africa is examined in a later chapter.

The widespread desire to add to armies inherited from the

colonial period by the acquisition of navies, where appropriate, and air forces, cannot be attributed to the prestige factor alone. There are real senses in which air patrol, and, if necessary, intervention, may be seen to be more economical than a network of army units on the ground. Anyone who has any knowledge of the prodigious—in terms of distance—task incurred by the Reconnaissance Squadron of the Nigerian army in trying to maintain some control of the frontier with the Cameroons immediately before and after independence, will fully appreciate this point. The success of the minute volunteer police air wings in Kenya and Northern Rhodesia is also evidence to this effect. Countries like the Sudan, Morocco and Algeria cannot be accused of military aggrandizement just because they acquire and expand air forces. Island countries like Ceylon, Madagascar and Cuba clearly have an innocent case for naval expansion. Generally, the more tenuous land communications are—and in Africa and Asia they are generally poor and focused on a few ports—the better the case for a tripartite defence force than for a traditional army on its own. The urge to acquire specifically trained airborne forces, notably paratroops, can be similarly justified, but because of their surprise guerrilla capability they are generally viewed with suspicion by near neighbours.

The circumstances of new states in a troubled world now suggest that the realization of dreams of true pacifism with no armed forces except for detachments within the police force will rarely be attempted. It is not the so-called 'cold war', so much as local rivalries and inherent instability which require the establishment of forces of a reasonable size; they may indeed be the prerequisite of peace. It is worth recalling that this aspect received little attention in the period before the avalanche of independence began with a landslip in 1957. On January 5 in that year there appeared, however, in an editorial in the journal *West Africa*, the following passage:

> In one respect the new West African countries are more favourably placed than most of those in Europe, many in Asia and even the United States. They do not have to squeeze their taxpayers for the astronomical cost of the appalling paraphernalia of modern warfare, nor are they saddled with debts incurred in

previous wars. . . . Independence does not greatly alter this, though it does mean some extra costs.

In the ultimate sense this has proved true, but the facts of relative stability, of remoteness from the world's flashpoints, and of the absence of really rich prizes in the way of resources, which were adduced as evidence at the time, are less significant than they were.

It is clearly a cliche to assert that the acquisition by new countries of the technical and other paraphernalia of nation states is all right provided it is kept within reasonable limits. This indeed is what seems to be happening, largely because of the stern controls imposed by a degree of financial stringency unknown in developed countries. The balance can, however, easily be upset by outside intervention. Foreign aid ruthlessly applied can quickly give one country a pre-eminence which in its turn almost inevitably leads to an arms race. This is the danger posed, for example, by the Russian decision to help Somalia to quadruple her forces in a way that can only appear as a threat to her Ethiopian and Kenyan neighbours. It is generally true to say that political leaders in most new states, which are not the recipients of a massive military boost of this sort, still need to justify, to the masses of the people and more especially to themselves, expenditure which they would strongly criticize in others. They not infrequently do this by asserting that military service can play an important role in nation building; whether this is an argument of expediency or a determining principle requires further examination.

V

Armed Forces in a Social and Nation-Building Role

SERVICE IN THE ARMED forces implies discipline of some kind, in all but the poorest military organizations, and discipline creates cohesion and perhaps a real sense of *esprit de corps*. Soldiers are brought together in a tight community with a clear cut set of rules which tends to smooth out personal and group differences and make human relationships conventional. Unlike most other professions, the military affects directly not only the serving men themselves but also their families, in that they too are often brought together in the contiguity of the military camp and subject to some discipline. Depending on the scale of recruitment, the army in a new state can thus play an important role in nation-building.

The incidental daily professional contacts are generally reinforced by an insistence on a common language of communication and instruction; these help to erode the tribal and racial differences which are an especial danger in new societies. In India, for instance, where linguistic divisions have resulted in violence and there are many different peoples, the army is to some extent a national melting pot in which the regional pressures are reduced in such a way as to make some fusion possible. In the Indian forces, however, while the officers all speak English, there is a relative lack of linguistic uniformity amongst the other ranks. In most other ex-British and ex-French territories the language of the imperial administration has been accepted as the official language and is to all intents and purposes common after the recruit stage. In Ghana the aim of early training is literacy in English, the language of instruction and command, and the use of native languages is officially prohibited; this is a policy which is demonstrably consistent with the demands of modern nationalism.

In no country have the national potentialities of the armed forces been realized more clearly than in Israel. In that small and politically isolated state a new meaning has been given to the term 'citizen army'. In many ways the Israeli experience is unique and some would argue that to use it as a point of reference in a discussion of the role of the armed forces in newly independent states is misleading to the point where it may invalidate lines of argument. Israel has some of the attributes of a Western developed nation and yet remains in other respects underdeveloped. It is nevertheless a 'new' state in the real sense of the word—that is, it is essentially an artefact built on the foundation of a single rock, which is the unity of the Jewish people whatever the cultural surroundings in which they happen to have grown up. In its creation, the army has been a principal and conscious agent which the leaders of the Jewish state have deliberately employed to fill a national purpose.

Although, until recently, the Jewish people have been in no position to organize a national army of their own because they were without a state, they had been forced to develop a capacity for resistance to oppression of the most extreme kinds. Some of the Zionist leaders like Chaim Weizmann also conceived, at an early stage in the development of the movement for a Jewish state, the use of a Jewish military contribution as a means of securing the support of countries like Britain whose international cause it might assist. Jewish contingents in fact played a part in both world wars but in the event the political effect was limited and subsequent developments in Palestine ironic. The tradition of self-defence which had enabled the Jews to survive through the centuries had also allowed the early immigrants to Palestine to maintain the integrity of their settlements. A system of defence based on the village unit worked adequately until the British assumed responsibility for the administration of the League of

Nations mandate. In the same way as, a century earlier, they had firmly discouraged the unofficial Boer Commandos in the frontier districts of the Cape, so in Palestine they were unwilling to tolerate a local 'freelance' defence organization. The British Palestine police took over the role which the Zionists had hoped their battalions might perform. However, in the face of Arab attacks in the late 'thirties the British authorities were forced to recruit Jewish soldiers for guard duties and night patrols, which the then Captain Orde Wingate played a major part in organizing. Though the war itself had a temporarily mollifying effect on the situation, there were in existence by the end of it three Jewish para-military organizations, the Haganah, the Irgun Tzvai Leumi and the Stern Gang, all dedicated in parallel but different ways to the creation of a Jewish state. These forces all played a militant role in the last days of British responsibility. With the withdrawal of Britain, Haganah, in particular, was forced to assume the defence of those settlements which were left at the mercy of the Arabs and the task of developing into a national army capable of fighting a war of survival. Preparations were made before the actual termination of the mandate in 1948, to equip it with up-to-date weapons, not only in the small arms range. The result was that when the government of Israel was established on a pro-visional basis, it had the nucleus of national defence forces at its disposal; but these had been created in such a way that they were also potentially capable of political domination. The various military formations were for the most part absorbed into the Israeli army, but dissidence caused the government to take strong action to disarm, in particular, certain of the Irgun elements. This action and the subsequent reorganization of the command structure was sufficient effectively to orientate the Israeli army within the framework of the state, and to ensure its control.

Since its inception, the main preoccupation of the Israeli state has, understandably enough, been the absorption of immi-grants. The task of acculturation has been to adjust to completely new conditions new arrivals from forty different countries who in total have outnumbered the 'native' Palestinians by almost three to one. The army of Israel[1] is made up of a small regular nucleus, a

[1] *Facts About Israel*, Ministry of Foreign Affairs, Information Division, 1963, pp. 70-3.

substantial national service force and a large reserve of trained men and women. As has been described, the army was born largely out of the Haganah organization and today the Defence Service law provides for all men between eighteen and twenty-six to do two and a half years' service and all women two years'. Minority groups are catered for by arrangement with the communities concerned; Druses and Circassians are by request actually integrated into the national service scheme, while Arab Moslems and Christians are able to volunteer. After full time service is complete, men and childless women are on call, up to the ages of forty-nine and thirty-four respectively, and are liable to a diminishing period of annual training which is increased for officers and NCOS.

The army command in Israel is constructed on a territorial basis which links together chains of settlements in the frontier areas. Almost every aspect of 'a nation in arms' is fully exploited to develop national sentiment. Not only are the age groups continually brought together but there is little evidence of cleavages arising from social class or background. Officers, who are far less clearly distinguished from their non-commissioned colleagues than in the traditional Western style army, are drawn from the ranks of conscripts and have no particular educational affiliations. There was a time when the key figures, especially in the Air Force, had a British or American wartime training background which made them distinctive, but today the only fissure which remains is between old residents and new immigrants, or between those from highly developed Western countries as compared with the arrivals from backward Asian, North African or East European areas. The newcomer has inevitable difficulties with the language and is more often unable to pass the advanced tests required for officer selection. Thus occasionally grievances may develop, but these are minimized by the careful control of officer status which is a feature of the Israeli forces; junior officers abound but there are few appointments high up the command pyramid, and these are methodically restricted to short tenure. Little distinction is made socially between officer and NCO ranks, thus making an interesting parallel with that prevailing in the settler community of Southern Rhodesia.

The most important feature of the Israeli forces, apart from their success to date in maintaining the integrity of the new state, is their educational role. It is intensive to the extent that, by comparison, countries like Britain may be said to have missed the opportunities inherent in conscription even if their needs were not the same. The process of civic education has often begun in the 'Nahal' or Pioneering Fighting Youth which gives some military training and then assigns individuals to farming settlements in particularly dangerous areas, and the Gadna or Youth Corps run, on scout lines with naval and air sections, jointly by the Ministries of Education and Defence. The army's object is to provide the necessary basic Hebrew and some vocational education in order to hasten the process of absorption into the national society and to make possible social mobility by those who might have remained forever, because of cultural disabilities, at a lowly level in that society. This process has been well described in civil as well as military terms by S. N. Eisenstadt.[1] It might be argued that the retention of a language like Hebrew is an expensive quirk in the modern world but if one language had to be chosen it at least had the virtues of history (though it may be worth noting here that it has proved something of a limiting factor on the range of Israeli plans for aid to Africa). All soldiers are taught Jewish history and essential geography, some of it practically in the course of extensive route marches round the country. Common military experiences for recruit groups extend later to farming, road building, tree planting and land reclamation.

In fulfilling its educational purposes the Israeli army is not dependent upon civilian resources. It has its own radio station, publishes its own journals and text books and generally acts as an educational institution—a projection of the national educational system. There are not many countries in the world where army camps are 'hives of cultural activities', but this is true of Israel.

The integration with civilian life of the military arm in Israel is discernible in other ways. Civilian support is essential to it and the normal ancillary services like medical aid, transport and supplies are not the subjects of separate military organizations.

[1] S. N. Eisenstadt, *The Absorption of New Immigrants in Israel*, Routledge and Kegan Paul, London, 1954, especially pp. 181 et seq.

Israel is not only 'a nation in arms', it is a nation which is organized in the expectation of war at any time. Israel's young senior officers are, however, not career soldiers in the full sense; they frequently step sideways into comparable civilian pursuits where their high level of general education and their technical skills are in demand. But the army does not only contribute to civil development through ex-servicemen, it takes a full part in society at all times. The refugee camp organization, for instance, owed a great deal to military ideas on hygiene and general administration and, as usual, swift aid has been forthcoming on the occasion of natural disaster. The Ministry of Defence joins with other agencies in the conduct of research and development to the extent that the Uzzi submachine gun and a new design of mortar have contributed to export earnings.

So far, Israel has managed to remain a civilian state and on the whole civilian values, on equality for instance, have permeated the army as much as military discipline and other attributes have done everyday life. This is partly because the army is not regarded as a profession apart but as an integral element, perhaps the most important, in nation-building, and has managed to remain unaffected by party politics. The effectiveness of the civil-military relationship and its clear social purpose raise the question of Israel's conscious inculcation of such a concept in the minds of new nations. In Ghana, in the Ivory Coast, Western Nigeria, Tanganyika and Uganda, amongst other territories, there has been a good deal of Israeli activity. In some cases her advisers have clearly had to damp the ardour of the leaders of new states in respect of the adoption of that unique institution the 'Kibbutz'. Assistance has been given with the diversification and improvement of agriculture and with co-operative retail organizations. But it is in the field of youth and para-military movements that Israelis, apparently with some reluctance, have come to make their most considerable mark. Inevitably the volunteers who work on these schemes have had military experience; one thinks particularly of the team of advisers who reorganized and reorientated the Builders' Brigade in Ghana and had a hand in giving it a new name—the Workers' Brigade—and links that achievement with the establishment of the Black Star Shipping Line and the elementary training of air force pilots before the RAF took over.

Is Israeli influence clearly discernible in the philosophy behind the social role of the armed forces in Ghana? Or are superficial similarities in treatment mere coincidence?

Certainly speeches by President Nkrumah at military ceremonies suggest that one reason for the expansion of the armed forces is to enable more of the youth of the nation to experience life in disciplined surroundings. Kofi Baako at a speech to the Accra Press Club in June 1963 also spoke on this theme. The army and navy volunteer forces in certain towns have been expanded alongside the development of civil movements like the Young Pioneers, once, however, compared proudly in the *Ghanaian Times*[1] with the Hitler Youth! There is no doubt that Ghana suffers like almost all developing African states from the problem of the half-educated unemployed city dweller who has been uprooted from traditional society and will need eventually some substitute for its restraints and responsibilities. In such circumstances the army may well be the one agent which can establish firmly the necessary standards of conduct, and so influence other organizations. During 1961, a number of officers of the Workers' Brigade attended a short course at the Ghana Military Academy, not only in drill and discipline but also in current affairs. These are 'straws in the wind' but the employment of the armed forces in a social role implies expansion, if any considerable number are to experience the advantages of its environment. There are, however, incidental, rather than deliberate, social benefits which can accrue from military service, which the absorption of Ghana's army in Congolese affairs, and more recently in providing an internal security presence, has tended to make less apparent in that country than in others whose awareness of the possibilities may actually be less.

In countries like Nigeria, Sierra Leone and Kenya it is natural for the army to come to the aid of the civil power in more senses than strictly for the maintenance of internal security. There are frequent natural disasters which only the military may be equipped to cope with on an emergency basis. Floods on a large scale are a case in point, when bridgebuilding and light air transport become of paramount importance. Such events, however, do put a premium on equipment of a kind which new

[1] October 12, 1960.

countries cannot readily afford, man or maintain. RAF helicopters deployed in late 1961 to assist the Somali Republic in such circumstances were the first ever to be seen in the hinterland of that country. It may be that the acquisition of a small air force can be justified in some cases on this ground alone. Bridgebuilding to isolated villages, as in Northern Nigeria, is a useful exercise in normal conditions, so is the clearance of obstructions to navigation on stretches of the Niger Delta. Lions or elephants even in parts of West Africa can become so destructive that they require mass armed intervention to deal with them. All these uses for the armed forces serve to bring them to the notice of the public and, if successful, rapidly infuse a measure of respect whatever the previous attitudes in the district. But there are other subtler and in the end more comprehensive ways in which the military can play a part in the 'modernization' of a state.

It is easy for the inhabitants of fully developed countries to talk of modernization in terms of 'civilized standards' and to mean by this freedom from corruption and impartiality in administration. Not infrequently, when one reflects on the scandals in police and local government and the 'expense account' mentality which affect even a country like Britain, there is a hint of hypocrisy in such talk. Standards, however, can be considered at a rather lower philosophic level. It might well be argued that reasonable hygiene is more important than the total abolition of 'customary gifts'. The armed forces can, however, play a part in both processes. A recruiting system, which is largely proof against bribery, however devious the methods, sets a good example and the disciplined community of the married soldiers' regimental lives can be a point from which the lessons of hygiene, anti-malaria precautions and so on radiate outwards into surrounding village society. It also provides an ideal background against which to tackle infant welfare and the problems of adult illiteracy amongst women. The conscious seizing of these opportunities in new states can make an important contribution to the attainment of national ends. Even in states so comparatively undistinguished as Persia, Peru and Paraguay, this has been realized at different times. In the last named country the army was for a time the chief instrument for economic development, and was actually responsible for the opening of mines and foundries and the construction of roads and canals. In Peru, the military is not only to some extent still a colonizing force bringing the remote, inaccessible mountain areas under the control of the central government, but at the Military College the officers are deliberately prepared for a socio-political role; and specifically for the organization of the continuous literacy campaign. In Persia today there are army 'development' battalions, but unfortunately the social advantages of these are largely offset by the top heavy defence budget which in its turn stems from defence forces which are, at 200,000 men, really too high for the country's immediate needs.

It is notable that it is in Pakistan that the army has emerged in a politically constructive role which provides one of the best examples of defence forces used to social ends. Some might compare this with the position in Egypt, but there are important differences and these spring in part from the fact that in that country the new army officer is drawn from the lower middle class, whereas in Pakistan he more often comes from the large land owning group. In Pakistan, some of the senior officers were, in fact, able to demonstrate their commitment to the new regime by giving up sections of their estates during the land reform programme in the early stages of the military administration. The army's initiative was, however, inspired by the contempt felt for the cumbrous and corrupt bureaucracy—a sentiment which included the administration even of the civil hospitals in Lahore. It was also directed against hoarding, the perversion of the rationing system and smuggling. The whole attitude of the military law administration was towards the cleansing of the state both literally and figuratively; the puritanical element appeared strong. On a single day it was reported[1] that a man had been fined Rs.1,000 for 'throwing rubbish and litter at a public place', and that, at Multan, one Ghuilam Haider was sentenced to five lashes for smoking in a cinema. In Mymensingh, the military sub-administration formed a welfare committee to improve the sanitation and the general appearance of the town. Local cinema halls, formerly dirty, were to be renovated, and Girl Guides were mobilized to 'preach among the housewives' the merits of keeping houses neat and clean and not buying 'surplus things

[1] *Dawn*, November 7, 1958.

55

which are not required for the time being'.[1] In Karachi, a sweet merchant was arrested under Military Law Regulations on the complaint of two army officers; the accused had dirty hands and when the officers drew attention to this he made 'uncalled for remarks' against the present regime.[2] At times, military enthusiasm for reform got out of hand to the point where General Ayub Khan had to withdraw the more junior ranks back to barracks to avoid a complete stoppage of commerce. Battalion commanders were reported to have thought up bright but impracticable ideas for collecting arrears of income tax and increasing production in local factories. Great attention was paid to enforcing respect for the national anthem when it was played in public places. The lack of a good civil service, most of the British legacy having been inherited by India, was Pakistan's main weakness; the vacuum provided the opportunity for the army to adopt a dynamic role in a policy of national reconstruction. This was not unlike the position in the Sudan, although in that country fear of a 'sell-out' to Egypt had been an important spur to military action. In most other countries, the armed forces, though an important social influence and 'yardstick', exercise an indirect control only and are perhaps barely aware of their nation-building potentialities. The army in Pakistan has been able to reconstruct the nation largely because of its ability to avoid compromise arising from political pressures. 'The key to the army's success was the strict discipline and blind obedience to the orders of their superiors'.[3] This has applied not only to serving soldiers but to ex-servicemen. The Governor of West Pakistan, Akhtar Husain, in a speech at Rawalpindi[4], described how in his view the training and discipline obtained in the army enables them to guide and lead the masses. 'By acting on the principle of self-help they can serve as models for others. They possess organizational capacity.' The army has been the instrument for spreading anti-tuberculosis treatment and education; it has also taken the lead in the promotion of new local industries. Pakistan's army, unlike that of

[1] *Dawn*, November 14, 1958.

[2] *Dawn*, December 27, 1958.

[3] General Haq Nawaz, addressing gazetted staff of the Karachi Administration as reported in *Dawn*, November 23, 1958.

[4] *Dawn*, May 17, 1959.

Israel, has gained its strength from a policy of exclusiveness and detachment; in a sense this is the reverse of the nation in arms but it has still been able to achieve a social purpose, by leadership rather than by permeation. Some might compare its achievement with the rule of the Major-Generals in seventeenth-century Britain; others would maintain that because of the wisdom of the man who is President it has avoided the excesses of that regime. The social role of armed forces in new states depends to a large extent on the degree of political stability, but it is also closely connected with the nature of the national leadership elite and its standing in the eyes of the masses.

VI

Popular Attitudes to Military Institutions: Defence Expenditure as a Political Priority

TO SOME EXTENT, THE ability and willingness of nationalist leaders to recognize the value of armed forces and, if necessary, to expand them, depends upon their assessment of the popularity, or otherwise, of the military element in society; but generally they will be at least as much influenced in their decisions on defence expenditure by other considerations of political expediency. An effective army, and eventually a navy and air force, may be one way of creating a national and international image of a 'modern' state. In domestic affairs, however, public opinion or popular prejudice is likely actually to determine the standing of the security forces in society, the respect or fear or contempt with which they are regarded and ultimately, therefore, their role in delicate political situations. The role played by the majority of the army in the successful rising in Brazil at the end of March 1964 clearly indicated the existence in the public mind of a military stereotype connected with a determination to uphold the constitution; this had been earned by long periods of apparent political detachment. Even in the longstanding Latin American 'new' states, such stereotypes are subject to change. This is much more the case in newly independent countries like those in Africa where the colonial period is a matter of very recent history.

In most parts of the world colonized by the great European imperial powers, notably Britain and France, the soldiers of colonial forces were regarded with a mixture of respect and fear; at the same time the army was generally regarded as a satisfactory and respectable career. The British Indian Army enjoyed a high reputation with most Indians, with the exception of the most politically conscious, in spite of the recruitment policy of drawing on selected 'martial' races. In British-administered areas through-out the world, the separation of the military from the police function in internal security was an important factor in maintain-ing 'respect' as the dominant emotion. Even where the general reputation of the soldier was in some way marred, the pressure of adverse economic circumstances almost always ensured an adequacy of recruits. Popularity and a flood of applicants to enlist have not been necessary concomitants.

Attitudes to the armed forces change as the political situa-tion develops. The effect of the second world war on the evolu-tion of public reaction to the armed forces in those states which have since become independent was of great importance. It is true that in the Indian subcontinent somewhat ill-informed Con-gress politicians had taken an active interest in the army in the early 1920s and that in French-speaking West Africa the issue of conscription had been linked with demands for citizenship rights, but generally up to 1939 the colonial defence forces were accepted unquestioningly as part of the imperial establishment and as a source of prestige and relative prosperity, particularly in those peoples or tribes from which the men were drawn. The war and expeditions overseas enhanced the importance of the soldier and gave him experience of a kind which was bound to affect civil-military relations. Demobilization brought with it, as it often does, discontent, and subsequent independence converted the forces into national institutions.

The shifts of opinion which can occur in little more than half a century are well illustrated in the history of British West Africa. Africans were first recruited in Gold Coast Colony at the beginning of the century and there was for some time a poor relationship between the army and the public due to its employ-ment in the police function of attempting to control petty thieving from European houses. The first world war, service in

East Africa and praise for the Gold Coast Regiment from General Smuts seem to have ensured soldiers returning from the campaign in 1918 a tumultuous reception in their home villages as well as at the ports of arrival. Even in Ashanti, the people's 'ingrained dislike of the regiment' was temporarily overcome, but resentment against the army was still to be found in that area in 1960. It was to many people a living reminder of the Ashanti loss of military sovereignty and, in particular, of the loss of prestige and authority by the chiefs who were once the active military leaders of the people. Young Ashanti are still conscious of the old traditions and not infrequently refer to the titles held by their male relatives in the military hierarchy of the Asantehene. The attitude of the central government of Ghana to regional and tribal loyalties has, of course, contributed to the maintenance of this local pride and resentment.

In Ghana, the distinction between the army and the police is clearly understood. In Nigeria, however, because of the greater size of the country, an army of similar proportions is inevitably less widely known, and confusion with the police, who are in turn popularly regarded as being unnecessarily violent, is, therefore, more common. Local anti-military prejudice exists, for instance, among the Egbas of Yorubaland. Here as elsewhere in West Africa, however, the 'glories' of independence have blurred the memories of unsatisfactory military behaviour in the demobilization period. Just because ex-servicemen were prominent in the political upsurge between 1946 and 1949 they did not at the time automatically become heroes. In Ghana, on the other hand, a few casualties have been made 'the martyrs of the revolution', but the mass were often regarded as malcontents disturbing the traditional order of society, while the regiment itself remained a symbol of foreign rule. This is an attitude which dies slowly after independence and only full local control can eventually completely obliterate it, if its achievement is at the same time accompanied by a deliberate publicity campaign such as that mounted by the party press in Ghana.

Where traditional sources of power and authority remain effective, they have still a part to play in moulding popular attitudes. In Northern Nigeria, the influence of the Emirs is still crucial in this respect and in recent times political considerations have led them deliberately to encourage the army as a career. In remote as well as in more populous areas all over the continent of Africa, the army has also come to be regarded as a useful refuge for those whose family ties are weak as well as for those who are keen to weaken or break them. But there is sometimes also a racial element in this complex of values. In Northern Nigeria, the army may be a source of livelihood for the Hausa speaker but still be generally rejected by the Fulani aristocrat as beneath his dignity. In Sierra Leone, the contempt of Freetown's Creole population for the Protectorate Africans has affected the army's status; nowhere else has the soldier been more emphatically designated 'an ignorant illiterate', though even there, efficiency in preserving lives and property, as shown in the Freetown riots of 1955, has served to modify contempt.

In Africa and throughout the underdeveloped world, the economic status of the soldier is fundamental to the standing of the army. There are few areas now where the outward signs of a good income are not an important status factor. This has its disadvantages, for it means that the profession of arms is more likely to be regarded as a job than as a vocation. The acceptance of danger, even though life may be cheap, and the endurance of hardship are not necessarily admired. The idea that to join the air force was suicidal stupidity was surprisingly prevalent in Ghana after a single flying training fatality. In East Africa, attitudes to the armies are coloured by the detachment preserved for one reason or another by major tribes, like the Baganda and the Kikuyu, from military life during the colonial period. The outlook of the Kamba, the heroes of the King's African Rifles in the Mau Mau period, has naturally become somewhat confused now that men of their tribe are, in the Kenya army, the servants of a predominantly Kikuyu government.

Though popular attitudes are influential, there comes a point in the history of new states where the leadership of opinion by the politicians is more important than the spontaneous expression of viewpoints which are no longer clear cut. The early development of a coherent foreign policy into which defence requirements are integrated is not a commonplace, but the desires to take up an apparently neutral stance and to acquire the essential paraphernalia of statehood have often combined with some realism in regard to practical military needs to transform the situation. In Africa the speed of political reaction has varied. Dr Nkrumah's speeches from 1959 onwards have constantly reiterated the theme of the security services as national institutions, and his own precarious survival probably owes a good deal to his handling of the army in that period. Julius Nyerere actually anticipated 'uhuru'[1] in his recognition of the army as a national institution, though the enduring effect of his action in this respect is open to doubt. In Kenya, it has not been easy to break people of the habit of regarding the regiment as identified with the imperial establishment. The British base, the presence of British troops and reliance on them for ancillary services, even in the Northern Frontier Province in the war with the Somali raiders, have all served to confuse the issue. In Nigeria, thinking on the subject of the defence services, as well as of the control of the police, has been affected by inter-regional rivalries. Ministers in the north have made no secret of their determination not to accept the presence of a federal army potentially inimical to their interests. The West, for different reasons, has been cautious in its attitude to the forces. In Nigeria more than in any other African country, the political potentialities of the armed forces seem to have been appreciated before independence. All the principal Nigerian leaders commented at one time or another on defence arrangements from this point of view. Dr Azikiwe, for instance, before he became Governor General, is reputed to have been interested in the establishment of an Institute of Military Science at the University at Nsukka and generally to have supported rapid Africanization in the army. The others took a less positive view, none more than Chief Obafemi Awolowo, formerly Premier of the Western Region and leader of the Federal opposition, whose trial in connection with an alleged plot caused a sensation. He gave full expression to his opinions in an autobiography[2] published just before independence:

[1] Swahili for 'freedom' or 'independence'.

[2] Chief Obafemi Awolowo, *Awo*, Cambridge University Press, London and New York, 1960, p. 307.

. . . our defence policy should aim at doing no more and no less than maintaining and modernizing the Queen's Own Nigeria Regiment in its present size and strength. There has been a great clamour in recent times for the enlargement of our army and our navy (such as we have) and for the establishment of a strong air force. Whom are we arming against, ourselves or our neighbours? It is often overlooked that these things cost a lot of money. Nevertheless it is my candid view that as much of these demands as are from time to time compatible with the preservation of our territorial integrity should be met. But we must not set out to build up these forces for mere national aggrandizement, or as an instrument for maintaining a totalitarian regime in Nigeria. The Dominican Republic spends fifty per cent of its total annual revenue on the armed forces in order to bolster up Trujillo's dictatorship. This will not do for Nigeria. Any government that does not enjoy the goodwill of the people should resign; it must not utilize the people's money both for the purpose of their enslavement and starvation. At the moment we have no need for considerably enlarged armed forces. Our people are peace-loving; and our immediate neighbours are friendly. No territorial claims have been made to our soil, and present trends suggests that no such claims are likely to be made to our soil in the foreseeable future (I am sure that we on our part have no evil designs on our neighbours either. Reports that one of our neighbours is making attempts to subvert constituted authority in Nigeria must not be discounted. But the surest way to frustrate such attempts is the prosecution of sound domestic policies which redound to the general well-being of our people.)

The implications of this statement are clear and were briefly developed by Chief H. O. Davies in a book[1] published in the following year in which he wrote, apropos the breakdown of democracy in other countries:

A large and efficiently equipped army constitutes an alternative ruling elite to the politicians, and the army is as much interested in stable government as any political party. If the government is threatened with collapse through maladministration of the politicians, the army cannot be expected to endure the ensuing chaos passively. It is ready and eager to step in and fill the vacuum.

[1] Chief H. O. Davies, Q.C., *Nigeria: the Prospects for Democracy*, Weidenfeld and Nicolson, London, 1961, p. 76.

Chief Davies, therefore, favours small armed forces for Nigeria.

The employment of considerations such as those quoted as seemingly relevant to the Nigerian situation was, however, really a political luxury and it is questionable whether they would be used in such a simple form now that the harsh realities of independence are more fully appreciated. The strict criterion against which the acquisition and size of armed forces ought to be judged is that of national survival: how far are they necessary for the maintenance of the country's integrity? To this the following corollary might be added: can the necessary expenditure be justified in relation to other priorities when account is taken of the nation's comparative poverty?

As an extreme example, the Israeli case for defence forces and expense expenditure is clear. When Israel came into existence a state of war already virtually existed. In fact, when the Arab-Israeli war began there were not even any defined frontiers. The result has been what seems a disproportionately expensive defence establishment, though the geographical facts speak for themselves. To quote a recent book,[1] sponsored by the Anglo-Israel Association: 'Israel's land boundaries total 590 miles, and against every mile (with the possible exception of the forty-nine miles running with Lebanon) are hostile Arab peoples, or at any rate, territories of hostile Arab rulers some of whom make a habit of threatening the extinction of Israel by force of Arab arms.' But Israel is an extreme, a unique case; the existence of no other new state is threatened in quite this way; no other small new state has similar historical reasons for its determination to survive nor the resources with which to do so.

Judged by practical considerations alone, the needs in the military field of most recently independent states are those of internal security with an occasional glance at an uneasy frontier. In theory a police force with well armed mobile elements should suffice. In the territories of former British Africa these already exist. The effective difference between the Kenya General Service units specially trained on military lines for mobile riot work, and similar forces in Northern Rhodesia and elsewhere, and normal infantry units, is unimportant, especially where, as in

[1] D. R. Elston, *Israel: The Making of a Nation*, Oxford University Press, for the Anglo-Israel Association, London, 1963, p. 77.

the two cases quoted, they are supported by light aircraft reconnaissance. The maintenance wherever British influence has been paramount of a clear-cut operational distinction between police and army has probably had an important bearing on the emphasis on separate military expansion. This is in contrast to the Francophone areas where the tradition of the *gendarmerie* is strong. The maintenance of the French connection for the purposes of defence has also restricted local military aspirations on sound economic grounds. With these facts in mind, it is curious that it was apparently only in Tanganyika and Sierra Leone that the disbandment of military forces was seriously discussed; it remains to be seen whether Gambia, whose future is still indeterminate, will decline to reconstitute even the company of infantrymen which was once recruited within its boundaries.

In so far as police forces attract a high proportion of the funds set aside for security expenditure and are generally considerably larger than the armies, their existence conditions to some extent the political decisions which are taken as well as the possibilities of *coups d'état*. Unfortunately, with some exceptions like the British South Africa Police in Southern Rhodesia, they are not well documented and information about them is difficult to obtain. Because of their closeness to the people in village sub-units, their difficulties may well be greater in the early period of independence than those of the more detached armed forces. They have to be able to speak the same language as those in the area for which they are responsible without being actually involved in local affairs or too strongly connected by ties of kinship. They are exposed to personal pressures and have to bear the brunt of unpopularity after punitive military intervention.

International prestige apart, perhaps the disinclination to rely exclusively on a police force arises from the problem of control. While the concept of a national centralized command for the army will rarely be challenged, because there is no practicable alternative, decentralization of police control may become a means of asserting regional autonomy and reflects local jealousies and rivalries. The effect may be to hamper prompt action by the central government in the event of an emergency. The elaborate arrangements which have to be made to meet these difficulties are well illustrated by the provisions of the Nigerian constitution. The Nigerian police are a federal force under the general direction of the prime minister and the operational command of the inspector-general. The prime minister himself presides over the Police Council on which sit ministers representative of the regions. While this council takes decisions on major matters of policy, staffing and recruitment come under the independent Police Service Commission. In operational matters, the officer in command of a regional force can appeal against instructions from the regional government direct to the Federal prime minister and Governor-General. In the Western Region there are also Local Government Police and in the Northern Region fifty-six separate native administrations have their own forces. The total strength of the Nigerian national police is 13,000 as compared with 8,000 military.

The fact that the police forces in East Africa remained unaffected when the armies mutinied in January 1964 raised important questions. The departure of three hundred Tanganyika police from Dar-es-Salaam to assist the new regime in Zanzibar appears actually to have cleared the way for the events at Colito Barracks. The apparent superiority of police morale has been attributed to the closer identification of the forces with the new states and this in turn may derive from the fact that, unlike the colonial armies, the police were specifically tailored to suit the needs of each territory. The armies of English-speaking Africa are a natural legacy of inter-territorial command organizations, which would be a useful factor if, for instance, East African Federation became a reality. The police forces, though under common Colonial Office direction, were able to develop local characteristics. Local, rather than remote Whitehall financial control meant a more rapid response in the way of revised conditions of service; this in itself could account for the differences in behaviour between the two kinds of security forces in East Africa. But all this and the suggestion that the Ghanaian and Nigerian police, because of the suitability of their training and experience, made a greater contribution to stability in the Congo than any military detachment has not convinced the politicians that the economy of one force would compensate for the loss of prestige involved. Nor is this a situation peculiar to Africa; even in the

West Indies, under the wing of the American defence system, the idea of the local regiment has been revived and steps taken to put it into effect.

Considered in terms of practical needs and international status, the decisions to retain and develop military forces are acceptable. Can the same be said of the acquisition of navies and air forces? Islands like the Malagasy Republic and Ceylon and countries with long coast lines like India have little need to justify their aspirations to sea power. Nigeria has been able to justify her navy by its anti-smuggling activities in the Bight of Biafra; Malaysia certainly needs a larger force to counter Indonesian piracy in the Straits of Malacca. More difficult to explain, except in terms of prestige, are the ships acquired by countries with short coastlines, such as Ghana, or with few maritime interests like the Sudan and Ethiopia. Presumably every country wishes to be able to make at least a gesture if the right of access to its ports appears to be threatened and few of the successor states have succeeded in building up navies obviously out of proportion to their reasonable needs. Indonesia is a possible exception, but the wide arc of islands which comprise the Republic President Soekarno is endeavouring to hold together raises doubt even in her case.

In these days, however, it is the acquisition of jet aircraft or, in rare cases, guided missiles, which arouses the suspicion of aggressive intention. Israel has grounds to fear Egypt's employment of German rocket experts and Malaysia Indonesia's stock of Russian bombers, but again there are few imputations of motive which can be readily proved. Lack of adequate communications is a characteristic of undeveloped countries which, when combined with long distances and naturally difficult terrain, makes a national air force reasonable and logical. For those with long frontiers in open or desert country, the air patrol may well be the most economical form of defence and, if the aircraft are suitable, the ability to deal with natural disasters is greatly enhanced. Such provision does, however, make great demands on the national economy in two ways; it cuts down drastically the funds available for social needs and, less obviously, tends to drain the generally tiny reservoir of technically trained manpower and, therefore, increases dependence upon foreign aid.

Only an exhaustive comparison of the educational systems in the new states could fully illuminate the second point, for only a few countries are comparatively well off in this respect. Indians, for instance, managed by the time of independence to acquire some engineering experience; Israel can call on the expertise of immigrants from all over the world or at least on temporary assistance from Jewish communities elsewhere, but large countries like Indonesia and Nigeria, with essentially peasant economies, are bound to find themselves in difficulties. In Africa generally, and especially in Tanganyika, Nyasaland and Somalia, higher education is an innovation; even in the relatively sophisticated society of Ghana with its long history of contact with the outside world, educated prejudice against training and employment in practical, technical fields is only slowly being broken down. In any case, the world demand for science teaching has weakened the secondary schools' ability to provide the necessary background. The difficulties, moreover, of introducing peoples to technological problems when their children have little acquaintance with elementary mechanical devices are generally underestimated. The role of the clockwork toy, the bicycle and perhaps the air rifle in the development of .defence science cannot be arbitrarily dismissed.

While priorities in the employment of educated manpower call for forms of planning which new states would find it difficult to enforce, they are all familiar with the question of financial priorities. Before the Chinese attack, the Indian government frequently asserted its preference for defence by social progress as opposed to the multiplication of armaments. The military crisis which has largely nullified this policy has produced an unforeseen threat to the series of development plans as well as bringing the risk of inflation through a rapid expansion in purchasing power.[1] In a country like India, however, which manufactures a reasonable proportion of its own armaments, military requirements could have a stimulating effect on heavy industry. Similarly the rapid training in minor technical skills of large numbers of recruits could eventually be beneficial to the economy. The effects of military expansion, without the urgency of

[1] For an examination of the economic implications see Barbara Ward, *The Plan Under Pressure*, Asia Publishing House, Bombay, 1963.

threatened invasion, in most other new states are likely to be quite different, with or without large subventions of foreign aid. Hardly any such states possess any relevant industry so that the additional expenditure does not greatly stimulate the country's economy. Increased taxes serve to postpone the day when large scale local capital formation, an important step towards economic independence, becomes a reality.

In India, the 1963–64 defence budget amounted to £650 million, which was about double that of the previous year and compares, for example, with the probable Indonesian figure over the same period of about £150 million. Though clearly the minimum defence requirements for small countries adversely affect the proportion of their defence budgets to those of large political units, the figures in the new states generally range between five and twenty per cent of the national expenditure, with the majority in the ten to fifteen per cent bracket. A useful guide to an understanding of the problem is that an infantry battalion organized and equipped on British colonial lines with between six and eight hundred men usually costs, in Commonwealth African countries, with the minor ancillary units necessary to its maintenance, from £1,000,000 down to £600,000 a year. This is a considerable deterrent to expansion for a poor country like Tanganyika whose government is normally unable to raise more than a total of £25 million for annual expenditure for all purposes. The establishment of a navy and air force is inevitably a costly matter. Two or three squadrons of unarmed aircraft, with facilities and training for officers and men might well cost nearly £20 million over a period of five years. This is the sort of proposed expenditure which in Nigeria seems to have inhibited what otherwise might have been considered a desirable development. Without massive aid, such as that apparently provided by the Russians for Indonesia and the Somali Republic, new states are not of themselves capable of large-scale military expansion. The curbing effect of financial stringency is such that only a rare leader will be able to maintain military expenditure at the expense of curtailing much publicised development plans; in Ghana, for instance, recurrent annual defence expenditure for 1960–1 was estimated at £4.5 million. For 1961–2 the figure was raised to £12.2 million, but was subsequently cut back, not to meet the criticism of the isolated opposition member who wanted to prevent the required increase in taxation, but apparently to maintain the momentum of the economy at a difficult time. Even the original estimate, however, amounted only to slightly under fifteen per cent of the recurrent expenditure planned. The typical new state in ordinary circumstances rarely has a planned target of an army of more than divisional strength including armoured car squadrons and a few parachutists; this is not the stuff of military aggrandizement and demonstrates very clearly the ultimate influence of hard economic facts and perhaps a genuine respect for peace. The arguments used to advocate the formation of a joint African defence force are not all concerned with aggression against South Africa; there is some reference,[1] from different quarters, to the heavy financial burdens implicit in the maintenance of national defence forces.

Armed forces in all their variety may for the time being seem necessary to new states for the sake of national prestige, if only to make a show for visiting dignitaries, but they are recognized as disproportionately expensive and there is some reason to hope that, provided great power interference is restricted, a national balance will be achieved in most parts of the world. This will free more resources for public works, national airlines, and new highways which, though immediately irrelevant to national need, and expensive, do usually make some direct contribution to social development, if only by way of fostering a desire for modernization.

[1] See, for instance, the speech by President Nkrumah to the National Assembly in Accra on January 20, 1962, quoted in *Ghana To-day*, January 31, 1962.

VII

Recruitment and Composition of the Non-commissioned Ranks

ALL ARMIES WHICH HAVE derived their present existence from a past incarnation as Colonial defence forces bear the marks of what in most cases was a clearly defined recruitment policy. This policy was generally based on ulterior political motives and sometimes reflected human prejudice on the part of the particular imperial agents. But even such a prejudice was probably conditioned primarily by preconceived notions of what was consonant with the security of an empire. There is no fundamental flaw in the generalization that, where there was any choice, British officers generally preferred the volunteer mercenary native soldier, especially if he happened to be both a Moslem and illiterate. French administrators were more ready to consider and advise conscription, but were no less inclined to prefer men whom they conceived as born warriors. The concept of 'martial races' was not the prerogative of the British in India, but the effect of their Indian experience was nevertheless profound.

At the time of the Indian mutiny of 1857, the East India Company's army consisted of a high proportion of men drawn from the Madras and Bengal presidencies, and of the Bengal contingent three-quarters had their origins in the higher caste families of Oudh. The conclusion drawn from the Mutiny by, for example, the Peel Commission, was that the Bengal army was too homogeneous. There was thus an increasing tendency to divide caste against caste and religion against religion. 'Our main object,' reported the Army Commission of 1879, 'is to make the army safe.' Systematic attempts were, thereafter, made to construct a reformed army in small segments; in other words, to form class units of battalion or company size and counterbalance them on every station and in every formation with natural rivals. At the same time, as already described in Chapter II, the balance of recruitment shifted and Nepal, the Punjab and the North West Frontier Province were systematically combed. The combination of 'efficiency with loyalty', which became the cry, was epitomized in the Gurkhas. Punjabi and Gurkha battalions were increased and in 1890 four Hindu units were actually disbanded and replaced by a combination of Punjabi Mussulmen, Pathans, Dogras and Gurkhas. Lord Roberts himself at this time had[1] a clear order of preference for the recruitment of reliable soldiers, viz., (1) Gurkhas, (2) Dogras, (3) Sikhs, (4) Punjabi Mussulmen, (5) Jats and Ranghurs and (6) certain classes of Pathan. At this period the Hyderabad contingent was only half local, the remainder being recruited in Northern India, and there was a general distrust of Eurasians. As time went on, memories of the Mutiny faded but were replaced by apprehensions about nationalism. The class composition of the army had encouraged to some extent its isolation from the people, uninfected by the contagion of political consciousness. K. M. Pannikar once suggested[2] that the army was, in fact, not national but 'an instrument of sectionalism in internal politics'. This is more difficult to confirm and it is not easy to accept the view that the elaborate regimental organization to keep in touch with pensioners in the recruiting areas was a blatant device to check the growth of nationalist opinion.[3] The disproportionate representation of particular groups was, however, clearly a danger to the new state and the balance in the case of the Sikhs, as officers at any rate, has been redressed since independence.

[1] Hira Lal Singh, op cit., Chapter III.

[2] K. M. Panikkar, Problems of Indian Defence, Asia Publishing House, London, 1960; New York, 1961, p. 28.

[3] Ibid., p. 50.

In 1957, the Defence Minister, Krishna Menon, was able to write:[1] 'We have to some extent reversed the processes of provincial bias which obtained in the army, especially in provincial units, state armies, etc., but other factors have to be guarded against.' In practice, the martial classes remain the main source of other rank recruits and the contempt for 'babus'—the educated classes—in this context, which the British to some extent cultivated, still remains. Thus, in India, a recruiting policy designed to meet an imperial crisis and to secure a flank when, for instance, the Russians were felt to be rampant north of the Himalayas, stayed on to create problems for independent India at a time when in any case the country was having to tackle the difficulties inherent in linguistic divisions. It could well be argued, however, that as far as the infantry was concerned, this policy served to make easier the partition of the army when in 1947 India and Pakistan went their separate ways.

The same policy, which, when applied in India possibly for the wrong reasons, may yet be said to have produced incidental benefits, had literally tragic consequences in Burma.[2] The effect of suspending Burmese recruitment for a period after 1925 was to give the Burma Rifles a tribal and community rather than a national allegiance, though at the same time it did achieve a remarkable solidarity and cohesion as between all ranks below that of King's Commissioned Officer, and even an exceptional loyalty towards the long standing European in that capacity. The divisions and antagonism were enhanced during the Japanese occupation, during which the hill tribes played a prominent part in the allied effort and the Japanese-sponsored Burma National Army was exclusively Burmese. As a result of the eventual agreement between Aung San and Lord Mountbatten, the Burma force was organized on a class regiment rather than on a class company basis, and initially consisted of five Burmese battalions and one each drawn from the three main minority peoples. Increasingly the nucleus inherited from the Burma National Army established political links with the government.

The seeds of dissidence were thus sown during the pre-

[1] *National Herald*, February 15, 1957: article entitled 'Public Administration—Federalism and National Unity'.

[2] For historical details see Chapter II.

73

independence period. In February 1949, all British officers in executive positions having been dispensed with at the time of independence, the regular Karen units mutinied and there can be little doubt that the role of the Karen colonels was decisive in bringing about the disavowal of the authority of the legal government. Throughout the troubled period since that event, the Burmese government has been forced to rely primarily on units raised on a racial basis, but has attempted to preserve the long term objective of mixed units as more conducive ultimately to political stability and professionalism. This has been achieved, to some extent at any rate, in the officer corps.

The development of the armed forces of Malaya has been subject to the same philosophy as that which Burma experienced by transference from India, but without similarly emphatic results. In Malaya the instigators of the concept of a native military force on a peninsular rather than on a local state basis were the rulers themselves. The question was first officially discussed in the Federal Council at Kuala Lumpur in 1920 on the initiative of a group of notables including the Sultan of Perak. It was not, however, until March 1, 1933, that out of one thousand men, the first squad of twenty-five was selected to form the basis of an experimental company. Numbers of potential recruits rose out of proportion to the demand. Applications were sifted by District Officers who employed artificial, not to say arbitrary, methods to reduce their numbers to manageable size. Insistence on a minimum height and freedom from obvious physical disabilities accounted for twenty-five per cent of the total. After that, intelligence and athletic tests as well as an exercise in the use of a simple air rifle were used to assess adaptability. In practice, however, recruitment was restricted to the four Federated Malay States, and Perak men were in a majority in the first hundred. Recruitment was gradually extended to every state and settlement so that the regiment was, as a short official history[1] put it, 'at that time . . . the one unifying influence among Malays throughout the peninsula'. The social barriers of parochialism disappeared during the stay at the training centre at Port Dickson, and visits to each others' villages and homes became common-

[1] *The Malay Regiment*, 1933–47. Department of Public Relations, Kuala Lumpur, undated.

place. Exceptional care was taken by the authorities to meet Malay sensibilities and customs; marriage was encouraged and married quarters built to maintain morale and stability. But it is tempting to read too much into this success. This was a purely Malay affair and it took the emergency, and the energy of General Templer, to force an appreciation that nationhood for Malaya involved the integration of the Chinese and Indian inhabitants. It was to this end that the Federation Regiment was started in 1953, but the fact is that Chinese recruitment, except occasionally of potential officers, has never been brisk. As elsewhere in the Malaysian public service, the need for careful justice on the part of the senior Malay officers towards the other races is a responsibility which has so far been generally accepted. It is nevertheless a potential problem, though one which lacks, at least at present, the intensity of its parallels elsewhere.

It is no accident that African forces in Commonwealth countries also bear the marks of British Indian influence. This influence has perhaps proved to be even more marked in the military than in the civil field; while the organization of administration was affected by the undoubted differences between the Indian Civil Service and the Colonial Service, the British military personnel operating in the two areas had almost everything in common and were frequently even the same men at different stages in their careers. Recruitment was, therefore, seen in the first place in terms of the imperial situation. Loyalty was the prime requisite and warrior qualities came to be identified with it. As times changed and some emphasis had to be placed on literacy and education generally, if only to fill the basic technical requirements of an infantry battalion, so the axiom came to be accepted that it was more effective to educate a fighting man than to militarize a soft ex-schoolboy. This was the theme, and the variations upon it from territory to territory varied with the tribal and political position.

Generally speaking, West Africans have not been unwilling to accept the role of the mercenary soldier. A soldier's life is regarded as providing steady employment, in a society in which it is not easily obtained, and a standard of living above the average, along with the possibility of a 'position of trust', if only as the licensee of a petrol station, after a career of moderate distinction in the ranks. Traditionally in the colonial Gold Coast the soldier was an illiterate from the North and often a Moslem. The theory that such a man was more reliable for internal security duties in the heavily populated areas was also accepted in the police, who along with the army at one time recruited extensively from the French-administered tribal areas to the North. As recently as 1960, there was some allowance made in the Ghana Armed Forces Training Centre for the absorption of such men—a fact which reflects in the first place the practical vagueness of the boundaries drawn between African territories as a result of the European partition of the continent.

Though Ghana today is more recognizably homogeneous than most African countries, the regional and tribal composition of any organization cannot altogether be ignored. At the beginning of 1961, about sixty per cent of the army was still from the Northern and Upper Regions and the figure for senior warrant officers and NCOs with ten or more years' service was closer to eighty per cent. A comparison of these figures at that time reflected the fact that, since independence, general recruitment had been concentrated in Kumasi, and for technical specialists in Accra, but the swing of the pendulum from the hinterland to the coast has since been checked by the reintroduction of occasional recruiting safaris in the north, with a view to avoiding dependence on the ability of would-be soldiers to get themselves to the recruiting officer at their own expense, a weakness which had put a premium on those who had already been wage-earners in their own right.

Ghanaians for the most part consider soldiering as an occupation—rather than a vocation—offering good opportunities for education and technical training which can be turned to advantage in civilian life. Whatever the current nuances of recruiting policy, there is unlikely to be a shortage of recruits. Forty applications for every place in a recruit squad has been a not uncommon figure. The general enthusiasm for employment was well illustrated in September 1960 when, on the morning on which the relevant notice actually appeared in the press inviting applications from ex-servicemen for re-enlistment to form a new battalion, by nine o'clock there were two hundred applicants waiting outside the Records Office near the Ministry of Defence.

The situation with regard to the navy and the air force, though requiring much smaller numbers of men, has been more or less the same. The navy in its early days was able to insist on a West African School Certificate with three credits as a minimum qualification for ratings who were to serve in all but the most menial capacities.

The pattern of recruitment to the non-commissioned ranks of the Ghana forces has never been a political issue, but in Nigeria the tribal composition of the public services has, since before independence, been a matter on which informed opinion has been extremely sensitive. The census returns which appeared to show a shift in the balance of population from the north to the south were significant partly for this reason; they could have affected ultimately the regional quota figures for recruitment as well as the structure of political representation in the Federal Parliament.

In Nigeria, not only has the principle of ethnic balance been accepted but also a procedure for its maintenance. The government, especially the Northern element in it, and its professional advisers, have been its protagonists on the grounds that the imbalance which might follow recruitment in accordance with intellectual and other similar qualifications would involve political risks which the new state could ill afford to run. It is, of course, open to question whether proportional regional representation in the public services should be an inherent feature of a federal system. At present, the quota system provides for the Northern Region to be represented to the extent of fifty per cent of recruits and the Eastern Region and the Western Region by twenty-five per cent each. There are also built-in safeguards to prevent what may be termed 'nominal' northerners from being overrepresented; within the Northern Region there is a tendency to follow a system of provincial allocation which keeps natives of Benue, Kabba, Ilorin and the Middle Belt generally from diminishing the opportunities of those from the 'Far' or 'True North'. Special conditions actually prevent individuals from filling vacancies allotted to a region other than that to which they and their fathers are native. This affects particularly certain parts of the north, such as the environs of Kano City, where the number of southern immigrants, especially Ibos, as traders and in minor official positions, is still fairly high.

This recruiting policy is not by any means universally endorsed. Some maintain that a modern state should not require to seek an artificial ethnic balance; selection for the federal, services should, they say, be strictly on merit. There is still, they claim with justice, an excessive predominance in the army of northerners, diminishing a little with the passage of time, which derives from the recruiting policy of the colonial period which drew in men even from the fringes of the Sahara beyond Lake Chad. For present purposes, they argue, it is easier to train a semi-educated recruit than to educate an illiterate warrior and it would, therefore, be proper to establish a minimum standard of education. This could be done without any threat to numbers but, for one reason and another, it would probably lead, as it did originally in the officer ranks, to a preponderance of Ibos. An advantage would be the saving of time at present taken up with the education of illiterates. The engagement of fifty per cent of soldiers in practice only for a short period of years to some extent exacerbates the problem and reinforces the critics' line of argument, but a great deal depends on whether military efficiency or social and political purposes are allowed priority.

Rules or no rules, in Nigeria as elsewhere in Commonwealth Africa, numbers are no problem; in fact, special precautions have had to be taken to avoid bribery and substitutions during the course of the elaborate selection procedure, a procedure which can be said to have justified itself by the physique and reasonable morale of those eventually posted to units. At this point, regional characteristics assert themselves to create another form of dichotomy. Infantry soldiers are generally northerners; the specialist, administrative and clerical appointments are often filled by Ibos. The most elaborate scheme cannot wholly, in a democratic society, check the effects of individual inclination and relative ambition.

What was once an association of a small colony with a fairly large protectorate has become the State of Sierra Leone; in the process there has been an inevitable shift of power from the sophisticated Creole population of the capital, to the Protectorate Africans. This is a change that affects most aspects of the national life, but to give it undue importance leads to an over-simplification of the problems of Sierra Leone. Over and above the tendency of the Creole to despise the primitive life of the hinterland, there is a not unimportant rivalry between the two main tribal groups, the Mende and the Temne. Since the rising of 1898, the former increasingly co-operated with the government in Freetown until they had advanced politically to the point where they were actually able to control it. The Temne, on the other hand, have remained suspicious and disinclined to accept the authority of others. There are numerous other tribes, of which the most important are probably the Fula, Limbe, Korankos and Mandingos, mostly still illiterate and predominantly Moslem.

In the face of this situation, the small Sierra Leone army of barely 1,000 men seeks to maintain a tribal balance, without a fixed quota system, in raising its annual requirement of up to 200 men. It is still true that education is most readily obtained in the area around the railway line to Bo which is, in fact, largely Mende country. It has for some time been the policy to keep the Mende strength to about forty per cent of the total, though this proportion has occasionally been exceeded. The effect has been that Mende recruits have often had the benefit of a substantial secondary school education, which is provided fairly liberally, by African standards, in their area, while the necessary contingents from the small, though apparently militarily inclined tribes like the Fula and Limbe are generally illiterate. This is the problem of Nigeria on a smaller scale and it reflects as clearly in its own way the various facets of colonial policy, in particular the desire on the part of the former administrations to avoid recruiting too many sophisticated individuals into the security services. Creoles do not often enlist except to become officers and are not easily integrated. The whole situation is complicated by the Mende-Temne rivalry which is never far from the surface even within a sub-unit. In general, family influence is strong and the power of the tribal societies, like the Poro,[1] is apparently a factor affecting the daily life of the regiment.

Though the problems were related and the philosophy

[1] The society in which Mende adult males are secretly initiated and which to a considerable extent still dominates the life of that tribe.

behind military policy was the same, there were interesting variations of practical application in the former British East African territories as compared with those of West Africa. In Kenya, Uganda and Tanganyika alike, it was, and with certain modifications, remained after independence the normal practice to enlist men from designated areas. There was a difference of emphasis as between the Gold Coast, Nigeria and Sierra Leone, but in all three territories tribal balance was considered in proportion to population as a whole. In East Africa recruitment targets were based on the 'worthwhileness as soldiers' of particular tribes or language groups. This was, in effect, a quota system restricted to an approved range of peoples, from which for one reason or another there were tacit exclusions at different times. In East and Central Africa, at the beginning of the century, recruitment was naturally confined to those who proved most amenable to military discipline and most likely to remain loyal. This was simply another and readily comprehensible example of the 'martial races' concept in practice, but, as in Nigeria, so in Kenya and Uganda it led to difficulties, for the simple reason that the largest groups who were in effect ignored for recruiting purposes proved to be the quickest to absorb Western education and the most active politically.

According to figures given by the Kenya Ministry of Defence to the press[1] at the end of 1961, of nearly six thousand African ranks serving in the King's African Rifles, thirty-four per cent were Kamba, thirty-four per cent Kalenjin and other tribes including Somali, Rendille, Samburu, Turkana, Masai and Luo, amounted to thirty-two per cent. The Kikuyu were not even mentioned and their representation was negligible. This was only partly due to the Mau Mau emergency during which their recruitment was not unnaturally prohibited. In the police force also, Kikuyus at nine per cent of the total amounted at the time to not much more than half the Kamba. In the two years between the release of these figures and independence, attempts were made to redress the balance but senior other rank appointments and the many officers promoted from the ranks still, of course, reflected the contribution of historical accident and deliberate policy.

[1] See, for example, *Daily Telegraph*, 'The Congo Fear that Haunts Kenyans,' January 8, 1962.

Young Kikuyu, however, did begin to come forward for officer training, but this was not substantially able to mitigate the dangerous situation of a country politically dominated by a group which knows itself to be weakly represented in the security forces. It does not require explicit speculation to see some connection between this and the unrest in the Kenya forces which flared up in January 1964. Since then there seems to have been a tendency to encourage military recruitment from the Youth Wing of the Kenya African National Union.

There is, however, little evidence in the welter of theories which followed the mutiny at Colito barracks, Dar-es-Salaam, that the Tanganyika troubles were due to tribal rivalries. It is a fortunate aspect of that country's development that, though certain tribes have been preferred as soldiers, they are in no cases numerous or important enough in themselves to have a predominant political role. In any case, the progressive spread of education has tended to invalidate the old preferences. In Uganda, however, it was the Acholi who were traditionally most sought after as soldiers once Indian troops had been withdrawn early in the century. In 1961, extensive recruiting campaigns were organized in the Western parts of the country, but even a change of policy had not led to the recruitment of more than a handful of Baganda, whose kingdom has proved the focus for political activity. It was an interesting justification of the imperial policy of recruiting the remoter peoples that in the March 1961 election in Uganda political interest amongst the soldiers was reported as remaining minimal to the extent that their registration as electors and attendance at election meetings was generally reluctant. This, however, is incidental to the main argument that the composition of colonial defence forces was planned in accordance with criteria which, however appropriate at the time of conception, ceased to be valid as soon as self-government and independence rose above the horizon. The practical application of the policy in its turn was influenced by the professional ethos of the parent imperial army. The British army was not, however, alone in the field; the French in its own sphere of influence helped to determine the eventual development of states whose independent existence could not have been foreseen.

It is said that in the remoter areas of British East Africa the appearance of a military contingent used to arouse ill-founded fears of forcible recruitment,[1] but in French West Africa there was actually a tendency to confuse recruiting with selling into slavery.[2] The French conquest of large stretches of West and Equatorial Africa and the consolidation of their administration in that area would not, however, have been practicable without African troops in substantial numbers. Their chiefs acted as recruiting officers but conscription of a kind was tried at an early stage. Though this was used as an argument in the campaign for citizenship rights by the politicians, discrimination in pay and conditions against the African soldier remained until recent times. In many areas, especially in the Sara country of Central Africa, the military tradition was strong and it was here that the French found the equivalent of the 'martial races'. Such men still serve in the Overseas Army and soldiers from Chad were prominent in the force which reinstated President Mba as head of the state of Gabon after the abortive coup in February 1964. But the system of compensation and pensions was for long in-adequate and the grievances of veterans were the subject at one time of a special investigation. There was not until the 1950s any comparable welfare system to that established by the British in India. The net effect of French policy was a legacy reflected in the insecurity of the soldier and the veteran which has been manifest in the Togo Republic, Dahomey and Congo (Brazzaville), in recent years. The combination of conscription with voluntary service enabled the French to recruit massive African armies, but left to the new states who had not the money or the use for such forces large male populations who lacked a central dis-ciplined core to their lives. The cry of 'national units' raised by the military in Togo and Dahomey concealed frustrations of a more complex kind.

Colonial conscription in West and Equatorial Africa had long term implications which have yet to be fully realized. In poor countries generally, however, the armed forces can stand for a square meal and comfortable accommodation. The Chinese

[1] Lieut.-Col. H. Moyse-Bartlett, *The King's African Rifles*, Gale and Polden Ltd., Aldershot, 1956, p. 126.

[2] Virginia Thompson and Richard Adloff, *op. cit.*, p. 120.

communists have recognized this aspect of the army's contribution to the state; conscription is for three years and provides an opportunity for indoctrination and discipline which appears to make a contribution to stability in China's particular circumstances. By contrast, democratic nationalism has its penalties and, because its armies are not forged in the fire of revolution but peaceably taken over from the former masters, it cannot reconstruct them immediately in its own mould. In such conditions, however small the total military force may be, its capacity to magnify and perhaps exploit the fissile tendencies of the state remain.

VIII

Officer Corps: The Evolution, Composition and Attitudes of Military Elites

FROM SITUATIONS WHICH HAVE arisen in different circumstances, in Latin America, the Middle East, Asia and Africa, it is clearly apparent that it is usually the officer corps which determines the behaviour and attitudes of the armed forces. The relatively greater prominence of officers in roles of political leadership, in new as compared with older states, is as we have seen primarily due to the smallness of the ruling elite in emergent countries. The speed or lack of speed with which the localization[1] of the officer ranks has taken place and the procedure by which it has been brought about, may have a bearing on the subsequent role of the military leadership in the new state. In Egypt a change of policy in 1936 on officer cadet recruitment to the military academy led directly to the revolution of 1952. In both Pakistan and the Sudan, Moslem countries with a reasonably long military tradition behind them, the armed forces saw fit to intervene in the affairs of crumbling governments a fairly short time after independence. In India, however, which

[1] A term now commonly and conveniently used instead of, e.g., Africanization, to describe the gradual replacement in the public service of expatriates by individuals, of whatever race, indigenous to the territory concerned.

84

had a shared military tradition with Pakistan, the forces have remained genuinely apolitical in spite of some attempts to interfere politically with them. For this reason, and also because India remains the world's largest democracy, and as such, in a curious way, the West's recognized but not self-admitted champion in Asia, the Indian army makes an illuminating point of reference—a stable control group against which the changes of others may be seen. It should, however, be emphasized that amongst the twentieth-century's new states India, with Pakistan, was the longest on the road to independence after the goal of self-government had been recognized. There was time, as there has not been in most other cases where the inclination has also been lacking, to take defence seriously from a nationalist point of view, and to see the localization of the officer corps as an integral part of the struggle for freedom. The Congress party in India, though often pacifist by conviction, were concerned about these problems from an early stage. Thus developments in India over the forty years before independence illustrate phase by phase the shifts in attitude involved in the conversion of an imperial defence force into a national army; at the moment of independence, moreover, the completion of the process could easily be conceived. Elsewhere the phases have run swiftly into one another and the nationalization of the military arm has been a spasmodic process in which prestige, pride and expediency have been more important than planning and efficiency.

Localization: The Case of India[1]

In the course of a meeting of the Federal Structure Committee of the Round Table Conference of 1930, Mahatma Gandhi is reported to have said[2]: 'A nation that has no control over her own defence forces and over her external policy is hardly a responsible nation.' Though from time to time the realization that Indianization was subject to the needs of military efficiency was apparent, and there was talk of the necessity for neutral

[1] The author acknowledges with gratitude the consent of the Institute of Race Relations to the use in this section of material first published in Vol. IV, No. 2 (May 1963) of the journal *Race*, as an article under the title 'The Indianisation of the Indian Army, 1918–45'.

[2] Quoted in *Indian Armed Forces Year Book*, 1959–60, Bombay, 1961, p. 471.

guardians of peace for the sake both of internal security and of the frontier problems which would be inherited from the British, the desire for a rapid increase in the number of Indian officers was generally unashamedly nationalist and backed by the minimum of expert knowledge. The lack of expertise should not be surprising, for how was a 'political agitator' against the Raj to acquire it.

Whatever its nature, political pressure, sustained and renewed over a number of years, and the world war were the chief factors in India's relatively advanced state of military preparedness at the moment of independence; no other new country was so well prepared in terms of army officers for complete autonomy.

In the Indian army, it was inevitably the cadre of officers holding the higher commissions which caused problems with regard to Indianization. There had for a long period existed another cadre of officers holding an inferior type of commission issued by the Governor-General or Viceroy. These were the vcos—in some ways glorified warrant officers, who acted as intermediaries or interpreters in a wide sense between officers and men. The rank of *effendi*, established in the 1950s in the King's African Rifles, was derived from the Indian experience. The vcos commanded platoons and made it possible to reduce the number of higher commissioned officers in the battalion to about half that needed in an exclusively British battalion. In the East India Company's army there had been Indians holding the higher form of commission, but after the outbreak of the Mutiny in 1857 higher commissions in the Indian army were reserved exclusively for British officers until the period of Indianization began in 1919. Thereafter there was an intermediate period in which both British and Indian officers were commissioned. Thus the close link between this question and the political circumstances at any particular time was established from the first, and in fact remained until October 1945 when the principle was finally accepted that fresh regular commissions should be granted only to Indians.

Almost from the date of its inception, the Congress party displayed an intense interest in military affairs; though not, except in rare cases, such as that of Pandit Kunzru, based on real knowledge or practical understanding, such a concern has not been paralleled in nationalist parties in more recent times. The planks of this part of the Congress platform consisted of demands for an overall reduction of expenditure, the establishment of military colleges empowered to prepare Indians for King's commissions and, above all, the ending of what they felt to be the Indian taxpayers' excessive contribution to imperial rather than local defence. The first official response to these suggestions was the innovation of a special form of King's commission in 1905; this provided for command over Indian troops only and for the attainment of ranks no higher than that of a squadron or company officer. By 1914, however, nationalist demands were more insistent, and the need for large numbers of volunteers for service in Europe and the Middle East brought concessions in an attempt to conciliate the so-called 'martial classes' from which recruits were expected to come.

In 1917, the announcement of constitutional reforms leading to responsible government was accompanied by a declaration that henceforward a limited number of Indians would be permitted to hold King's commissions and that, to this end, ten vacancies a year at the Royal Military College, Sandhurst, would be allotted to Indian candidates. This established the principle of equal eligibility for command of British or Indian troops, which alarmed many senior British officers and at the same time intensified political clamour for a clearly defined localization programme.

The debate on the merits and dangers of Indianization was to continue for another two decades, but the stances which the various parties adopted were already substantially clear in 1919. The resistance of the existing expatriate officer corps to drastic changes seemed, as might appear normal in these circumstances, to be compounded of a subtle mixture of professional pride and a sense of racial superiority, in which the former element was probably predominant. The point of view expressed by General Sir O'Moore Creagh, a former Commander-in-Chief in India, was in certain respects typical. 'Indian soldiers,' he wrote, 'much prefer serving under British officers, for they refuse to believe those of one Indian race will, or possibly can, deal out even-

handed justice to those of another.'[1] He continued (p. 276):
'The weakening in leadership caused by giving King's Commissions to Indians must be reduced by being limited to people of war-like classes . . . it will preclude British officers from serving in the Indian army and on them its efficiency depends almost entirely.' On the other hand, Sir O'Moore Creagh asserted that the intimate knowledge which Indian officers possessed of the mental processes of the rank and file would prove a great advantage, but unfortunately, he felt, the proper social integration within a regiment would be prevented by the problem of officers' ladies from different races. The marriage customs of both Hindu and Muslim created obstacles, because (p. 278): 'English ladies do not care to associate with Indian ladies whose social position they do not know, which is not to be wondered at.' Such considerations led the former Commander-in-Chief to advocate the Indianization of selected units on a class-regiment basis, while at the same time suggesting that it would be unwise to insist on an English language qualification or to permit the entry of officer candidates 'from unwarlike classes' simply on grounds of political expediency.

The assumption of a basic distinction between leadership qualities on the one hand, and intelligence plus educational attainment on the other, was not unique to the Indian situation or to the particular period concerned. In fact, however, the ultra-conservative position in all these matters was quite rapidly eroded. A factor in beginning the process was undoubtedly the conduct of those Indian officers who had been commissioned by the end of the war and particularly of the four who had served in the Royal Flying Corps in France, one of whom was awarded the DFC. The rate of failure amongst Indian cadets attending Sandhurst was initially fairly high; of the eighty-three admitted to the RMC between 1918 and 1923, two died and the failure rate amongst the remainder was about thirty per cent as compared with three per cent amongst their British contemporaries.[2] (Of the

[1] General Sir O'Moore Creagh, *Indian Studies*, Hutchinson, London, 1919, p. 274.

[2] Report of the Indian Sandhurst Committee (the Skeen Committee), H.M.S.O., 1927, p. 10.

total entry thirty-five were from the Punjab and twelve from the Bombay Presidency.)

Political pressure, however, was sustained and eventually effective. On March 28, 1921, Resolution 7 adopted in the Legislative Assembly included the following clauses:

> that every encouragement should be given to Indians—*including the educated middle classes*— . . . to enter the commissioned ranks of the army . . . the large majority of the selections should be from the communities which furnish recruits and as far as possible in proportion to the numbers in which they furnish such recruits.[1]

A year later, in March 1922, the Prince of Wales Royal Indian Military College was opened at Dehra Dun with a capacity of seventy cadets, to provide an education on English public-school lines in order adequately to prepare young men for the Sandhurst course. The 'Admission of Indian Gentlemen to the R.M.C. Sandhurst' was now an established practice, and plans, however gradual, began to be made for full Indianization over a long period of years. General Cobbe in fact proposed at this stage the establishment of a separate Dominion Army destined eventually to replace the British Indian Army.

In most official quarters, proof of Indian efficiency was still held to be required. As already mentioned, some disquiet had been caused by the failure rate at Sandhurst, which the Prince of Wales College considerably reduced. The policy of full Indianization of eight units was adopted in 1923 'to test the practicability of successful Indianization in the Army'.[2] This scheme was criticized by the political leaders as implying segregation and as a result of two more comprehensive Assembly resolutions in 1923 and 1925 respectively, the Indian Sandhurst Committee was appointed in June 1925. Before reporting, its members visited educational institutions in England, France, Canada and the United States. With two exceptions, its membership was Indian; it included M. A. Jinnah, and Pandit Motilal Nehru who resigned in March 1926. The committee was charged with investigating the possibility of establishing a military college and improving the quality and quantity of Indian candidates for commission. A cautious foreword to their report described the committee as in

---

[1] *Ibid.*, p. 6 (author's italics).   [2] *Ibid.*, p. 9.

search of 'the surest line of advance towards the creation of a Dominion Army'.[1]

In evidence, Sir Malcolm Hailey (now Lord Hailey), then the Governor of the Punjab, and Sir Prabhashankar Pattani both stressed the imperial importance of a sound Indian officer corps. The ignorance of the educated classes about the army as a career and their reluctance to consider it, even when aware of the possibilities, is a recurrent theme of the report: 'sections of Indian political opinion charge the Government with having increased unnecessarily the difficulties in the path through the restrictions of the Arms Act, or, as political opinion expresses it, the disarmament of the people'.[2] The committee accepted the view that the military tradition needed to be more widely diffused in society and regarded the fact that the instructions to the selecting authorities implied a preference for the sons of soldiers as a deterrent to the achievement of such a state of affairs. Contemporaneously outside the committee the view was expressed that 'no attempt has been made until quite recently to associate with the Indian army the Western educated classes which British rule has brought into being'.[3]

At a time when in emergent countries the enthusiasm for an overseas education is great, the reluctance on the part of Indian parents in the 1920s to expose their sons to the competition and 'temptations' of Sandhurst may seem surprising. The risk of being, through failure, 'thrown upon the world without any marketable qualifications'[4] did not at first seem to very many of them to be worth taking. In the committee's view, however, appreciation of the value of a period of residence in a foreign country was increasing, though such experience would still seem expensive to the parent who had to provide a sum of between Rs.7,000 and Rs.11,000 to pay for it.

Other, especially social, difficulties in the way of Indianization, however, loomed large. A recently published book by Sir Valentine Chirol[5] had evidently, to judge by the report, made a great impact on opinion on this question. Chirol referred to:

[1] *Ibid.*, p. ii.   [2] *Ibid.*, p. 12.

[3] Sir Valentine Chirol, *India*, Ernest Benn, London, 1926, p. 277.

[4] Report of the Indian Sandhurst Committee, p. 15.

[5] Sir Valentine Chirol, *op. cit.*, pp. 277–8.

'belated concessions to Indian sentiment . . . the process is too slow and confined to too narrow a field to satisfy Indian impatience . . . the cry for Indianization which carries a special meaning for Swarajists who are quite conscious of the dangers that British withdrawal would mean for a "Swaraj" India with no "national" army behind her . . . Though the Army Department may wish now to approach it chiefly from the point of view of military efficiency, it has to reckon with the strong racial objections of British officers to being placed in the position of ever having to take orders from Indian officers.'

The report itself[1] referred to the harm done by a lecture said to have been given at Sandhurst, advocating the Indian army as a career and suggesting that British officers were insured against the risk of ever serving under Indians. It went on to say: "The average Indian parent is reluctant to destine his son to a military career, and feels that the Indianization of the army is, in the minds of the authorities, still suspect and uncertain.'[2] According to Chirol, the most important factors were, on the British side, the loss in prestige thought to be involved in submitting to Indian command, and, on the Indian, the aggravation to the situation caused by having to contribute heavily to the costs of imperial defence. Opinions and considerations such as these led the committee to remark that the 'eight units' scheme had evidently produced such a degree of suspicion and mistrust as to be almost irremediable without the cancellation of the plan. Unfortunately, direct evidence from units in which King's Commissioned Indian Officers were already serving, not only in the lowest ranks, is hard to come by, but it seems legitimate to suspect some exaggeration here.

At this stage, the development of an Indianization policy was clearly inhibited by other more practical considerations. If parents doubted official commitment to such a policy, then they were unlikely to destine their sons to a military career, while the authorities' proper insistence on the maintenance of the highest standards—the avoidance, in fact, of anything smacking of 'double standards'—itself inhibited the volume of recruitment and helped to encourage the doubts. Indeed it might well be argued that official insistence that Indians should be in every

[1] Report of the Indian Sandhurst Committee, p. 18.   [2] Ibid., p. 21.

respect replicas of British officers was *really* to maintain a double standard, since the act of carrying out duties in a foreign language and living in an essentially alien environment imposed exceptional strains, and was itself a handicap in striving to achieve the required standard. The establishment of the College at Dehra Dun, amongst whose products there had been no failures at Sandhurst, had established the value of an English public-school type education for leadership and character training, though West Point, it was claimed, was able satisfactorily to make up the deficiencies in this respect of American schools. The shortage of Indian schools with a suitable ethos was one of the weightier arguments in favour of a longer officer education in India than in Britain and, along with the danger of diluting Sandhurst (a maximum of five per cent overseas intake was then regarded as acceptable), part of the case for a local college. It is interesting to see here that British and Indian nationalist arguments tended to lead to the same conclusion, though it is not easy today fully to support the argument that 'this personality (of a college or university) would be destroyed or distorted by the influx of a large number of strangers'. Since 1947, the percentage average of overseas cadets at Sandhurst has often been nearly three times what was regarded as acceptable in 1925, without creating more than marginal problems.

The Skeen Committee, at the end of its deliberations, proposed amongst other things a target of fifty per cent Indianization by 1952. In March 1928, the Commander-in-Chief declared as Government of India policy the establishment of a national army corresponding to the development of full self-government. There was still uncertainty about the reaction of British officers to a wider dispersal of Indian officers beyond the eight units. There were now more coming forward than were required to fill the posts of King's Commissioned Officers in these units. It was argued by the British authorities that in the Indian Army of the future there would be no need for the vco who had served as a link between the men in the ranks and officers whose mother-tongue was English. The new Indian officers in the British Army should command platoons, and draw pay equivalent to that drawn by a British subaltern in his own country. This might have been accepted by Indian politicians had it not been for the presence of those officers commissioned into the Indian Army under the old system who did not command platoons and who drew higher pay. The politicians protested that this was discrimination and merely a device for delaying Indianization. Writing in 1928–29 from a definitely conservative standpoint, Sir Reginald Craddock[1] remarked on the danger that the Indian Army would disintegrate without British leadership, each group seeking leaders of its own race, caste and creed. Rapid Indianization he declared to be futile on the grounds that officers from martial races would not follow Congress politicians, and that men in their turn would not follow 'the non-martial intellectual officers'. This was not a national army—in a sense the soldiers were 'foreigners to the politicians'. Such points were highly debatable and can only be judged in long term by results. What was not disputable was that some aspects of the proposed Indianization, notably the replacement of vcos by commissioned officers, were expensive and calculated to reduce the opportunities for promotion.

The Defence Sub-Committee of the Round Table Conference, 1930, brought up the matter again and this time the Indian Military Academy was the outcome, though 'Indianization was still ostensibly an experiment only'. The need to recruit widely in order to canalize 'passionate feelings of national patriotism' which might otherwise find expression 'in anarchist and revolutionary activities and deadly agrarian and communal riots'[2] was recognized. Minutes by individual members of the Indian Military College Committee stressed the need in a federal state with autonomous provinces for the representation of all classes, and propounded the view that only fair and open competition would minimize communal rivalries. Some opposed the allocation of fifty per cent of all vacancies to cadets already in the Indian army, on the grounds that this gave preference to existing classes from which recruits were drawn. It was the opinion, for instance, of Dr B. S. Moonje that a quota system by provinces was required, and that the distinction between the martial and non-martial classes perpetuated a mercenary army and propagated communalism. Other Indian members of the

[1] Sir Reginald Craddock, *The Dilemma in India*, Constable, London, 1929.
[2] Report of the Indian Military College Committee, H.M.S.O., London, 1931, p. 40 *et seq.*

committee reviewed the whole history of Indianization back to the Mutiny, and attributed to political expediency many of the decisions taken. They quoted Roberts and Kitchener on the subject of the essential superiority of the British officer, and even John Galsworthy's play, *Loyalties*, to demonstrate the difficulty of producing a confident Indian officer corps in a force in which Britons predominated. They recalled, as evidence of official attitudes, Major General Tucker's suggestion, enshrined in the Peel Commission report of 1859, that it would be good policy to 'divide and so neutralize the strength of the castes and nationalities which composed our armies in the East', by dilution with Africans, Malays and Arabs. Experience of leadership was lacking, one minority minute suggested,[1] because a sense of inferiority to the British soldier had been deliberately inculcated. But by this time the horse they were flogging was almost dead. An academy producing sixty officers a year, whose terms of service were similar to those of their British colleagues, could no longer be regarded as experimental, whatever the theory, and was capable of conversion into a truly national institution.

Henceforward progress could be gauged statistically; by March 31, 1935, there were 150 King's Commissioned Indian Officers, and the first had successfully graduated from the Staff College at Quetta. During the same year, Kitchener College, Nowgong, was established to secure potential army cadets who were to be promoted from the ranks, and in 1936 an Army Class was started at Government College, Lahore. Many weak candidates were, however, still coming forward and the number of good candidates was not rapidly increasing. On October 1, 1939, when the Defence Department appointed an Indianization Committee, there were 396 Indians out of a total corps of 4,424 officers; the normal peacetime intake was 60 Indian and 120 young British officers. On the whole, the view of the Indian official history,[2] that 'before September 1939, Indianization of the

[1] Report of the Indian Military College Committee, H.M.S.O., London, 1931, p. 81.

[2] *Official History of the Indian Armed Forces in the Second World War, 1939–45*, 'Expansion of the Armed Forces and Defence Organisation', Sri Nandan Prasad, Ph.D., Orient Longmans for Historical Section India and Pakistan, Chapter XI, pp. 169–88.

higher ranks of the armed forces was the result mainly of nationalist demands' is substantiated, even though it tends by implication
to underplay the real concern for professional standards which
lay at the root of reluctance in some service quarters. 'But after
1939,' the official history continues, 'it was the Government
which put forth its best efforts to obtain Indian gentlemen for the
officer ranks of the services.'

Political opinions now affected recruitment dramatically.
Until the later promise of full self-government after the war, the
Indian National Congress policy of non-co-operation caused many
young men to refrain from joining the forces. The Hindu
Mahasabha, however, supported the war effort, while 'the
Muslim League adopted an intermediate attitude'.[1]

The immediate result of political reactions to a war from
which many Indians were inclined to dissociate themselves was a
sharp increase in the proportion of British officers. By the beginning of 1941, Indians were outnumbered by twelve to one, but
this was only a temporary phase. Three years later, the figure was
four and a half to one, and on September 1, 1945, four to one.
Many candidates were inevitably rejected, even in wartime, and
some were reported as lacking proper motivation. The official
history comments[2] on this point that a sense of service or patriotism was 'an ideal impracticable in the existing political set-up
of the country'. In spite of the personal efforts of Sir Claude
Auchinleck as Commander-in-Chief, in the face of some opposition from British officers, the final traces of racial discrimination had only been gradually eliminated; in at least one corps
Indian officers were only given disciplinary powers over British
personnel comparatively late in the war. How far such considerations and the unfavourable political atmosphere restricted
Indianization is now hard to judge. The fact remains that
by October 22, 1945, when the Government of India
announced that in future only Indians would be eligible for
regular commissions in the Indian armed forces, there was a
reservoir of 8,340 officers, excluding the medical services, out
of whom to establish a completely Indianized army; the most
senior were Brigadiers. It was on this basis that the officer corps
of India and Pakistan were built. In many respects it is regrettable

[1] *Ibid.*, p. 171.　　[2] *Ibid.*, p. 188.

that the lessons and experience of South Asia have not been consciously drawn upon more often in planning the development of new national armies during the decolonization of the 1950s and 1960s. It is indeed ironical, but for strategic reasons not surprising, that defence and the composition of the army should have been so much more a matter of political concern in an early than in the later examples of the transfer of power.

India : Officer Education since Independence

In the historical sense, India provides us with the classic example of an army for which at first the imperial power provided places at its own military schools, then established a local institution, and eventually on independence transferred complete responsibility to the new state. India, moreover, has subsequently modified the system to suit her own ideas on the integration of the three defence forces, and in so doing has borrowed from other sources, including the United States. This evolutionary process is worthy of examination primarily because it tends to demonstrate the acceptance by an Asian state of the Western European/ American concept of a professional army. This in its turn may be an indication that the choice of nation-builders in this respect is limited, and that great variations on the pattern of officer education as between armies are not normally regarded as practicable.

The clash between India and China in late 1962 caused a sharp disillusionment in India and focused attention on the Indian army and on the structure of the officer corps. The suggestion was made that the British pattern had been too closely adhered to, and that the result had proved to be an army unsuited for the conditions of Himalayan warfare; in some way the apparent failure was to be attributed to Britain, even though after fifteen years of independence the whole body of junior and 'middle piece' officers in operational units had been commissioned under national arrangements. The fact was that the Indian government had made only minor changes in the general policy of recruitment and education. They had, for instance, kept the two forms of commission, and had undoubtedly been aware that the reputation, international and domestic, of the force was due in the first instance to its record in imperial service. For this latter reason, the conscious conversion of the force into a national army closely integrated with the other institutions of the state had been pursued less thoroughly than might have been appropriate. To some extent this deficiency, if that is what it is, is well illustrated by the approach to officer education since 1947, which in its turn well demonstrates the difficulties of new states in endeavouring to create their own professional tradition.

The destinies of the Indian armed forces since independence have, needless to say, been under the guidance of men commissioned during the British period. Of the thirteen senior officers (general to major general) whose biographies appear in the Indian Armed Forces Year Book, 1958, all but one attended either RMC Sandhurst, or RMA Woolwich, after a period at British-type schools, and two had actually been to school in England. The first Indian engineer officer, commissioned in 1932, was in fact one of these. A similar pattern, though less complete, is discernible in the air force after 1929. A feature here and in the Indian navy has been the way in which the specialized military education has apparently fitted them to transfer towards the end of their careers into such appointments as General Manager, Hindustan Aircraft (Private) Ltd.; General Manager, Indian Air Lines; or Managing Director, Hindustan Shipyard. This flexibility in the deployment of highly educated military personnel in fields in which their skills are at a premium, is likely to be a widespread characteristic of administration in new states, even where the army is not in political control.

The new Indian government inherited the Indian Military Academy, which had been opened at Dehra Dun in 1932 on the pattern of Sandhurst. For some time after independence a strict conformity with trends in Britain, achieved by regular liaison visits, was maintained, until the establishment first of the Joint Services Wing at Dehra Dun in 1949, and then of the National Defence Academy at Khadakvasla, near Poona, which opened early in 1955. The College at Dehra Dun continued for some years to examine changes in syllabus at Sandhurst and often responded to them. The organization of the Defence Academy is, however, in some ways unique, and in others derived from the American pattern.

In 1945, before independence, a committee was appointed to plan a defence academy, and visited the USA and Canada as well as Britain. Their brief from the government was to establish an institution 'on the lines of the United States Military Academy at West Point'. It was on this project that the Indian government spent, in the first instance, the £70,000 with which they had been presented by the Sudan government in recognition of the services of Indian troops in the Western Desert and East Africa. The Academy, as finally established, provides for entry by merit, with pre-university matriculation qualification, at the age of between 15 and 17½ years of age, to a four-year course. Of these four years, three are actually spent with cadets of all three defence services at the Academy, and they then go on to their respective Service Colleges, in the case of the army, the Military College at Dehra Dun, for more specialist training. The official objectives are worth remarking; according to the Armed Forces Year Book: 'What it [the Academy] turns out is not "educated wage-earners in uniforms" but patriots with full realization of their duty as guardians of national freedom and the national way of life. . . . The portals of the Academy are open to all young men. There is no distinction or discrimination on the grounds of class, creed or religion. The Academy, in fact, is a meeting ground of young men from distant corners of the country, living and learning in utmost harmony, despite the differences in class, creed or religion. Living together, cadets start on the same footing and grow up in an atmosphere of a healthy secular outlook.'

In order to achieve all this, a strict discipline is employed, focused on the Code of Honour, and at the same time a wide range of cultural and sporting activities is encouraged. The emphasis in the academic curriculum is essentially conventional with the stress on science, mathematics and English. Some attention is paid to social studies, to Hindi, the nationally recognized Indian language, and to practical engineering work in the workshop. Throughout, and especially in the last year, the officer cadets' mess prepares the students for regimental custom and tradition. Thus is the Honour Code on West Point lines blended with British methods of achieving and maintaining *esprit de corps*. It is perhaps the fusion of traditions, on the one hand strictly professional, and on the other vigorously apolitical, which has enabled the Indian army so far to play a proper and unobtrusive role and to be a genuine force for national unity. It has contrived to create an aura of integrity, which has so far thwarted attempts by individuals in the Lok Sabha or lower house of parliament, for instance, to interfere with selection and rejection procedure.

Four years of intensive training and reorientation may in itself be sufficient to guide the young man on to an unswerving professional course from which he will not easily deviate. In these circumstances methods of potential officer recruitment may not seem particularly important. In fact, the Indian method corresponds to the British open competition as a result of advertisement, in which selection tests, both individual and group, play a prominent part. There are two main differences between the two systems. India relies much more heavily than Britain on the recruit from within the army and, like her neighbour and rival Pakistan, is enthusiastic for the idea of the preparatory military school. This is not simply a recognition that selection for officer training by psychologically scientific methods is not enough, that in practice eight or more years training are desirable rather than four; it is a realistic assessment of the problems of national unity in a vast society, with wide differences in wealth and culture. At one time, the British navy normally took in its officer entrants at twelve, and there are some who still hanker after this system even today. According to the Year Book quoted above, the Rashtriya Indian Military College, with its roots in the British period, exists for 'the primary object of catching "would be" officers of the Armed Forces at an impressionable age to be able easily to mould their character'. Great stress is placed on physical standards, self-reliance and social training. There are also in India four King George's Schools at Ajmer, Belgaum, Bangalore and Dagshai; one-half of the vacancies in each case are reserved for the sons of junior commissioned officers and other ranks and the remainder for those of officers and civilians connected with the forces. Institutions with a similar purpose are Sainik School, Nabla, which admits boys aged 9 to 12 to a course along the lines of an English public boarding school, and reserves 120 of its 200 places for the sons of ex-servicemen, and the Army Cadet College, Nowgong, opened in May 1960, to provide training for certain categories of youth, to fit them to appear before the selection board.

India's officer training schemes have apparently maintained the objective of an apolitical army, which is nevertheless an important educational and stabilizing factor in the state. If this has, in fact, been achieved, then the lesson is that in a developing country a long period of careful adjustments to professional standards and requirements may be needed if an officer corps is to resist political pressures. That the army in Pakistan has, however, taken a different political course may be an indication that in a Moslem state things are different, and that it is not the officers but the general political climate which is the final determinant of the military role. Most of the newer countries are not as essentially conservative in outlook as those of the Indian sub-continent, and have certainly not had the time in which to develop a professional ethos; for them the whole process of military development has been compressed to such a degree that the separate stages are not clearly discernible; it is for this reason that this aspect of what seemed at one time the interminable progress of India towards full independence has a special value and significance for the purposes of comparison.

Commonwealth West Africa

The Royal West African Frontier Force (RWAFF) owed much to Britain's Indian experience. The timing of its development from the 1890s onwards, and the fact that there were few British officers of the period who did not spend some time in the Indian sub-continent, combined, if not to impose a pattern, certainly to suggest what seemed tried lines of development. For a time at the beginning of this century, there were actually some Indians in the WAFF, and Lugard himself had received his military initiation in India. Even today Kaduna, now the capital of Northern Nigeria, closely resembles a typical Indian cantonment in the last days of the British Raj, the model on which its layout was in fact based. The influence extended to the question of personnel. The concept of warrior races, tribes or castes which it is easy today to criticize, was an inherent part of British military thinking as applied in Asia, the Middle East and Africa. It is not fanciful to suggest that Lord Wavell's difficulties as Viceroy of India lay to some degree in his preference for the apparently soldierly Moslem, and similar considerations have affected advice given by expatriates elsewhere, particularly in relation to Northern Nigeria. In every respect it was natural and not necessarily unwise to think of a gradual preparation of independence in West Africa along the lines which had been adopted in India. Indeed it can be argued with some justification that the relative stability of English-speaking West Africa as compared with other parts of the continent is due to the fact that these were the last new states actually to be prepared for independence, and that this was particularly applicable in the case of the army officer corps. The position in this respect of Ghana, Nigeria and Sierra Leone at the time of independence was certainly not as advanced as that of India, but it was infinitely better than that prevailing in Tanganyika, Kenya, Uganda, Somalia or the Congo.

The provision of African officers for the RWAFF did not become a serious issue until 1950–51 when the first sure signs of Gold Coast progress towards self-government were apparent. An African officer had actually been commissioned during the second world war in the Gold Coast Regiment, and reached the rank of major. He was later to be transferred to the Foreign Service, a career pattern which could prove a significant guide to future developments. Africanization of the officer corps was inevitably delayed, both until some experience had been acquired in other branches of the public service, and for another reason of considerable importance: a colonial force is an agent of imperialism and viewed with suspicion by the educated elements in such a society. It can only be made generally respectable by its recognition as such by the nationalist political leaders; this takes place only when the prospect of independence is actually in view. It is, however, possible that the adminstering authorities missed their opportunity with the well-disposed Gold Coast elite by the rule, for instance, which appears in the 1930s to have prevented individual Africans from joining University Officer Training Corps while being educated in Britain. Even if this is so, the effect of a different policy, in view of the numbers involved, would have been marginal and 1951 would have remained a significant date in Ghanaian history in the military as well as the political sense.

Today's senior officers in the Ghana army were all commissioned from 1950 onwards and to begin with were mostly drawn from the military education service. The senior warrant officers and NCOs from this quarter were virtually the only well educated men in an illiterate force drawn largely from the Northern Territories where education had not yet penetrated. Hence the predominant influence of the leading secondary schools near the coast, notably Achimota. From that time onwards the process of selecting and training potential officers gained momentum. From 1953, Ghanaians began to be admitted freely to the Royal Military Academy, Sandhurst, and to the two Officer Cadet Schools at Aldershot and Chester, which at that time offered shorter training courses. The assumption always seems to have been that a sound educational background and professional training of real substance would make a valuable contribution to the stability of the new state when it achieved independent status. It was always likely that sooner or later political pressures would produce a situation in which a crash programme became inevitable. Though there was a natural inclination on the part of British advisers to go slowly in the interests of thoroughness, there is little evidence that this substantially inhibited the development of an African Officer Corps in Ghana. In fact, the risks involved in gradualism seemed more often to have been expressed by expatriates than by leading politicians who were certainly not unaware of the dangers of creating rapidly a politically conscious army which would not have the opportunity for settling into a professional groove. This is a dilemma which has been well illustrated on the other side of the African continent in the case of President Nyerere of Tanganyika. In Ghana, the gradual process was allowed to continue for three years after independence, and then early in 1960 the decision was taken to establish a local military Academy at Teshie, near Accra. This was intended to accelerate Africanization and at the same time provide for the planned expansion of the force to the equivalent of about two brigades as well as for the basic training of air force and naval officers. By January 1961, about half the officers in the army were African. In September and October 1961, after Major-General H. T. Alexander, a British officer seconded as Ghana Chief of Defence Staff, and a number of other officers, had been suddenly dismissed following President Nkrumah's return from the Soviet Union, the pattern changed again. British officers ceased to hold executive appointments, and to meet the deficiency the course at the Ghana Military Academy was for the time being reduced in length. Since then, British military aid to Ghana has been renegotiated and now consists of a military mission of all three services—a formula which seems satisfactory to both parties. Ghana has at different times made use of training vacancies not only in Britain, but in India and for a short time, until the military coup there, in Pakistan. In September 1961, sixty-eight cadets for the services were despatched to Moscow, but it is not known how many are likely to complete what was projected as a three- or four-year course. By August 1962, forty-seven Ghanaian officers had been commissioned from Sandhurst alone, a figure which should be related to a total officer strength at that time approaching three hundred. Many of these are in key positions; one is a Brigadier and was, in fact, commander of the Accra Garrison during the troubled period before the Queen's visit in November 1961.

The typical professional Ghanaian officer is then a young man with secondary school education, and often trained in a military establishment overseas for a period ranging from about six months to nearly three years. Strict social generalizations are more difficult to make. At first there was a tendency for officers to come from prominent families with connections in other professions, but more recently their range of origins has been wider and to a large extent dependent on the chance of the right level of education. They are absorbed into the elite, but they are not necessarily born into it. An army officer is more likely to be the son of a peasant cocoa farmer or a post office official than of a professional man, who inclines to regard the Bar or the civil service, especially the foreign service, as having greater prestige.

By the end of 1960, there were two African brigadiers in the Ghana army, and by October of the following year all the senior ranks including that of major-general had been filled by promotion. Short of a rapid expansion of the army, now inhibited by financial stringency, the period of dramatic promotion opportunities is virtually over. The need for high quality officer material remains, but no doubt greater selectivity can be employed. What is more important to appreciate, however, is the actual significance for individual officers of the completion of Africanization. What follows can easily appear to the ambitious as stagnation. All Ghanaian officers are relatively young—none more than forty-five—and a great many of them in their middle and late twenties. The dangers of a promotion block were important arguments for gradualism at a time not long ago, when 1965 was still the target date for completion of the whole process. Cliques could readily develop and the nightmare vision of a conspiracy of "been-to" officers, of the kind which some people evidently thought would be uncovered by the Granville Sharp Commission of Inquiry, become a reality. Nevertheless it is true that in Ghana the fate of Major Benjamin Awhaitey[1] who was court-martialled for his connection with the plot which the Inquiry sought to investigate, seems to have played a considerable part in damping down political urges amongst officers, at one time to the point where every relevant conversational question received a non-committal reply. Correspondingly, the affair served to some extent as a deterrent from undertaking an army career amongst men of socially well established families.

European observers are inclined to expect in public services in Africa the growth of a sense of vocation at a speed which is really unreasonable. In new societies the criteria by which a career is selected may be more clear cut than in established societies; though it is true that in British and other European military circles family tradition is still an important factor affecting officer recruitment. Marginal decisions are taken in West Africa between careers on the grounds of what seem relatively insignificant differences in pay and perquisites. The matter-of-fact treatment of commissioned service as 'just another job' did not, needless to say, find favour with Britons brought up in an atmosphere where a certain militarist mystique is accepted. The establishment of a tradition which will give this sort of privileged group cohesion is not likely to be easy in conditions where social pressures, especially that of family obligation, are strong.

Another factor which provides an obstacle to this kind of

[1] Major Benjamin Awhaitey was found guilty at an Army Court Martial held in January 1959 on the charge of neglecting to report information about an alleged plot to kill or capture the Prime Minister on December 20, 1948. This led to the appointment of the Commission of Inquiry.

development is the inherent respect for age which has not made easy the relationship between ex-schoolboy officers and warrant officers and NCOs of long standing. This is a potent source of grievance, and it is interesting in this context to recall that for a time the police in Ghana tended to evade it, and often had cadets in training for gazetted rank, who, in fact, were sub-inspectors in their forties with a limited career in front of them. At the time of writing, however, in spite of all the problems and the political tensions of the country at large, there have been as few rumours of military disaffection—if one leaves aside the unique circumstances of the mutiny of the 3rd Battalion of Infantry in the Congo in January 1961—in the Ghana army as in any comparable African force. This may be partly attributable to the assiduous care with which the army has been cultivated by the President, but it owes a good deal to the reasonable preparation of the officer corps for its responsibilities. It could, it is true, be argued that the case of Nigeria is parallel, but in that much larger country the tribal factor has been the source of a certain uneasiness in all the public services, especially at the higher levels.

In what is now the Federation of Nigeria, the first African officers were commissioned a few months before their Ghanaian opposite numbers, but, whereas in Ghana overall command had been transferred to African hands by October 1961, a British officer on contract was still in command of the Nigerian army at the end of 1963. These facts can be interpreted as a true reflection of the greater impact of ethnic and group rivalries on the one state than on the other. For this reason alone in Nigeria a cautious approach to localization was explicable; an analysis of the origins of the more senior officers makes it more so, particularly when considered in the context of a thorough-going attempt to avoid a promotion block towards the end of the 1960s. The most senior Sandhurst-trained Nigerian, a northerner, reached the Royal Military Academy in 1952; by the beginning of January 1961 there were eighty-one Nigerian officers out of a total of more than three hundred. This was passable progress, but much affected by the composition of the elite group thus created. Nearly sixty of the eighty-one were Ibos from the Eastern region, and many of them came from a comparatively small homeland round Onitsha on the east bank of the Niger. This faithfully

105

reflected the uneven distribution of facilities for secondary education in Nigeria, as well as the local lack, for historical reasons, of enthusiasm in the west for the army as a career. The area bounded by Onitsha, Umuahia, Owerri and Afikpo in the east is not only an Ibo 'heartland', but contained in the 1950s more secondary schools than the whole of the vast Northern region. Later, in 1961, a regional quota system was introduced for officers as well as men and eventually the imbalance will be redressed, but in terms of rank structure at the top of the promotion pyramid this is bound to take a considerable length of time. In a federal state where stability rests on a delicate framework and complex interplay of forces, this is obviously a matter of considerable importance, especially when the Prime Minister and the Minister of Defence are from the Moslem north. The problem is to satisfy the requirements of political balance, and at the same time to preserve standards, as far as possible, on a national and impartial basis. If, however, only educational qualifications were regarded as significant for officer selection then in the early stages in this situation even the most ingenious quota system would be ineffective if other considerations were not brought to bear. In Nigeria, therefore, because of the educational advantage of the south, the pressure for Africanization when it has come to the surface has been largely from the southern element within the army; in other words, the retention of executive command by expatriates could be interpreted as directly thwarting for political reasons the achievement of high status by those whose education and training appeared to deserve it, a claim which in itself had its origin in tribal rivalry. A significant illustration of the tensions was the article which appeared in the *Sunday Times* of Lagos on November 13, 1960, suggesting that the chain of command in the Congo should be from the United Nations officer responsible directly to a Nigerian and not through expatriates whether in Lagos or Leopoldville. It should, however, be observed at this point that this was not a specifically military phenomenon, and that quite frequently at this period, in connection with civilian posts, demonstrations to the effect that '—— must go!' were to be seen in the cities of southern Nigeria.

The shortage of officers from the Northern region which, as has been suggested, is continually in the process of correction, will by its nature prove short-lived as far as numbers only are concerned. It is ironic to reflect that it is more or less directly due to the original Moslem opposition to Lugard's plans for the introduction of Western education in the north. This is a point which is well appreciated in that region and an active interest has, as a result, been taken by many of the traditional rulers in both secondary education and the specific military question. The Emir of Katsina's younger son was commissioned from Sandhurst in 1959, and the opportunities offered by the establishment of the Nigerian Military School at Zaria have been fairly fully exploited. This tackling of the problem from the ground upwards is an important feature of the attempt to raise officers, and is in itself almost certainly better than attempting to redress the balance abruptly by commissioning a large number of warrant officers and NCOs of long standing.

As was to be expected, the Congo operation brought about a salutary realization of the difficulties involved where tribal jealousies and the presence of expatriates are combined. To act in defence of European interests, as frequently occurred, against 'fellow Africans' was a delicate assignment. *The Times* of January 18, 1961, contained a full account of the problems of morale arising from the defence of an Austrian ambulance for which the senior Nigerian officer was, in fact, decorated by the government concerned.

Since 1961, the officer provision of the Nigerian army has been progressively stepped up, by extending the range of countries whose training facilities can be employed, as well as increasing the numbers of young men sent to Britain, especially for the short course of officer training available at Aldershot. Nigeria's links with Pakistan have also been developed, and at an early stage a senior officer was sent to the Quetta Staff College, while another was at Camberley. In addition, the development of a defence services academy at Kaduna has been planned in the face of difficulties arising from the expenditure involved in establishing an air force. Though for the moment the African army officer corps in the Nigerian army represents a sizeable proportion of the country's leadership elite, its expansion in direct relation to the growth of the reservoir of suitably educated men is unlikely. In terms of influence on the affairs of state, this probably means that the Nigerian officer and, therefore, the army is less likely to play a decisive role than they are in other new states. Three to five hundred officers in a country of forty million based on five main military stations, the majority of which are far from the capital, cannot for the time being be regarded as a political factor of the greatest importance. Indeed, it may be that the two elements, the small size of the forces in relation to population and area and the brevity of the officer professional tradition, will prove the ultimate determinants of the military role in African politics generally. The military do not represent an effective alternative to civil government in the same way as in the Middle East and South-east Asia. Until the local officer corps is at full strength and has had the chance to develop a real professional cohesion, this will remain true. It is likely that the fact that the mutineers in Tanganyika in January 1964 did not recognize power when they seemed to have it in their grasp is related to the virtual absence of an established officer corps. This deficiency in itself could, however, be a source of instability.

East Africa

As recently as the summer of 1962 it was possible to write,[1] as the author, in fact, did:

> The officer position in the forces of the three East African territories has been the cause of some publicly expressed anxiety in view of the achievement or the approach of independence. This is *much less marked in the case of Tanganyika* and less important in Uganda than Kenya.

The exception then accorded to Tanganyika was due to the apparently satisfactory stability of the country, to the relative absence of racialism and the initial response of school leavers to the invitation to apply for officer training. Unlike the police force and the civil service, the scale of the problem seemed small; fifty good candidates over a period of two or three years and, it seemed, the process would be complete. To a greater degree than in the case of the RWAFF, the King's African Rifles (KAR) had come to be regarded as a regional rather than a territorial

[1] William Gutteridge, *Armed Forces in New States*, Oxford University Press for Institute of Race Relations, London and New York, 1962, p. 47.

organization. The East African Defence Committee had overall responsibility up to the moment of Tanganyika's independence and Headquarters East Africa Command in Nairobi was a force headquarters in all respects. While the units had gradually tended to become indigenous to a particular territory, the supply of officers had been handled to some degree centrally. At the time when the provision of local officers was first considered, the territories themselves had, however, begun to assume militarily what seemed then particular social and political characteristics. Pre-selection of applicants was, therefore, arranged territorially and the final selection carried out by the command organization.

The results were in a way bizarre and significant of the lack of realism which has periodically invaded the politics of the three East African countries during the last five years. The essentially Ruritanian but potentially explosive situation in Uganda inhibited the emergence of educated young men willing to be officer candidates. Buganda youth clearly thought that there were too many hurdles to clear on their way to officer status, and saw many alternative routes open which would lead them to the proper niche in society which they felt to be their due. Other tribes had few men with the necessary qualifications. The result was that Uganda produced her first successful candidate for officer training at the end of 1959, and just two more as a result of the full selection procedure in 1961. Confidence that Tanganyika was proceeding along an unprecedentedly moderate path for Africa, and one on which multi-racialism would be acceptable, deprived the situation there of any sense of urgency, and led to the commissioning of the first non-European, an Asian, at the end of 1960 and then of two Africans via Sandhurst in 1961. Kenya, too, was assumed up to the Lancaster House Conference at the beginning of 1960 to be on the road to multi-racialism, and to this end a number of British officers were transferred to the permanent staff of the KAR, and several young Europeans commissioned into the regiment directly from Sandhurst along with an Indian and a Goan of Portuguese descent.

It was in Kenya, however, that a sense of urgency first developed and genuine disappointment was evinced at the failure of the recruiting campaigns. It is interesting in this connection to note that it was the promotion of the first African lieutenant-colonel in Kenya, and the determination to hasten Africanization apparent at the independence celebrations there which is said to have caused the initiation of a report on the subject in Tanganyika which was being urgently considered at the time of the mutiny at Dar-es-Salaam.[1] The situation in the Kenya force in fact came to a head in the course of 1961. Of the applicants from secondary schools who asked to be considered for Sandhurst in March 1961, only eleven had the necessary qualifications and only three, none of whom was successful even at the preliminary board, turned up for interview.[2] The implications of this state of affairs were realized in the ensuing months; the case of the Force Publique was frequently recalled though the parallel was not a strict one. By December 1961, eight effendis—platoon commanders similar in status to the Viceroy's commissioned officers in the British Indian army—had received the Queen's commission. At the end of that month the British government gave approval for a scheme to commission about thirty more effendis at once and to send substantial numbers of senior NCOs to Mons Officer Cadet School at Aldershot.[3] Pay increases were announced at the same time and by April 1963, eighty-four Africans or about half the officer strength of the officer corps had been commissioned in good time for independence. In this context, remarks made by Tom Mboya in the Legislative Council on African promotions are worth quoting,[4] referring to the early promotion of four African captains, he said: 'It is not a question of promoting captains overnight. We want an effective army and not a lot of pretty uniforms.' He was thinking, he said, of the need for attractive terms of service to draw in the best men.

The process in Kenya, however, was not so straightforward as the bare facts suggest. In the first place there was the tribal factor; such rapid promotion inevitably strengthened the position in the army of the non-Kikuyu element, for the simple reason that there were virtually no Kikuyu of any experience to promote and school leavers were still hard to come by and only provided a

---

[1] Keith Kyle, 'Mutinies and After', *Spectator*, January 31, 1964.

[2] *The Times* African Correspondent, December 13, 1961.

[3] *The Times*, December 29, 1961.

[4] Tom Mboya, *Freedom and After*, Deutsch, London, 1963; *Little Brown*, Boston, 1963, p. 157.

trickle for training in Britain. The potential effect of the tribal balance on the morale of the Kenya army will remain a danger for some time, especially when the role of the force in the colonial emergency caused by Mau Mau is recalled. There was also for a short period some racial tension created by the understandably slow adjustment to new circumstances by the civilian population. The Nanyuki European Club situated close to the brigade headquarters of the KAR had realized the implications of non-European membership of the officer corps and cancelled the block regimental mess membership to meet the situation. European officers resigned their membership of the Club in protest, and in December 1961 a Club motion to admit African officers to membership failed to get the necessary two-thirds majority. The *Times* African correspondent reported[1] that it was the recent urban European immigrants who opposed and the Kenya farmers of long standing who tended to support this motion. The latter have inevitably since prevailed but the whole incident was illustrative of the social complexity of attempting the Africanization of society at one of its most sensitive points. Those few but influential members of the short lived Federal administration in Rhodesia who actively advocated the recruitment of African officers may not have fully appreciated the revolutionary nature of the step which only the voluntary withdrawal of a successful African candidate for training prevented from being taken in 1962.

In Kenya, it was not only the comparatively trivial matter of club membership which hindered development. Great importance had been attached to a junior leaders company at Kahawa which was intended to form the nucleus of the elite of the three East African armies; boys of fifteen—a total of 150 of them—had been recruited with a view to their long-term education for officer and senior non-commissioned positions in the local units. In March 1963, they refused to obey orders and the 'mutiny' was only ended when Brigadier P. Sholto Douglas of the Tanganyika army flew to Kenya to address them. Eighty-three of the boys were eventually discharged[2] after there had been established evidence of political interference leading to a 'conspiracy of

[1] *The Times*, January 1, 1962.
[2] *Daily Telegraph*, April 3, 1963.

silence'. In anonymous letters of complaint sent to politicians in the three countries, they had complained of being called 'baboons' and 'monkeys' by European and other staff, and objected to the posting of an African officer after an adverse confidential report, as well as to relegation after failing to achieve the prescribed educational standard. This type of educational approach to officer provision has not had the success in Africa which experience in India and Pakistan has led some of its devotees to expect.

Tanganyika and Uganda were both affected by the 'mutiny' at Kahawa but had also in the meantime gone along with Kenya in the matter of commissioning non-commissioned ranks of proved experience. The process in each case could be argued as too fast or too slow; there is, for instance, little in the Somali experience of 'crash' localization within six months of independence to suggest the superiority of such an approach. The fact is that expatriate military advisers and local politicians 'cannot win' in this matter; speed and gradualism are both full of hazards in the Africa of the 1960s. To refer again to West Africa—Mr Matthew T. Mbu, Nigerian Secretary for the Navy, was once reported[1] as saying: 'It is the policy of the Federal Government to see that systematic Nigerianization of all key posts in the country's defence is carried out, because in time of hostility it is the indigenous officers who would be called upon to save the nation'; and he then went on to explain the plan to Nigerianize the army and the navy and to create an air force by 1965. These sentiments properly expressed the problem but in East Africa events have called the tune. When the Tanganyika Rifles mutinied at Colito Barracks under the leadership of a young education sergeant, the Ministry of Defence was already considering a plan initiated by British officers for the complete Africanization of the leadership, including the Brigadier's appointment, by the end of 1964. The captured cap of the British Commander was accepted, apparently under pressure from the mutineers, by the only African officer graduate. At the time, thirty-five officers in the Tanganyika army were African, some of whom were locked up with their British colleagues, as against twenty-nine Europeans, and unfortunately unknown to the rank and file plans

[1] *West Africa*, February 2, 1963.

already existed for the promotion of three to major and eleven more from the ranks. In Uganda, similar progress had been made. The apportionment of blame for what will continue to be a precarious situation would be both impossible and irrelevant; what matters is that, unlike in some ex-colonial countries, the creation of stable professional officer corps in East Africa is an added delicate responsibility for the political leaders in circumstances in which they would have been glad of such an established group as allies loyal to the state.

Officer Corps in Other Areas

Generally speaking the nature of the officer corps in the armies of new states is influenced by two main factors—their socio-economic status in relation to other elements in the leadership elite, and the educational standards expected of them. With this latter point is associated the question of the source of that education; in what tradition have they been brought up and alongside what alien army have they received their training? The influence of British or American or Russian or French training is a complex matter for separate discussion which affects not only the officer corps but the whole pattern of military behaviour, including command procedures, as well as arms and equipment. Amongst officers, long overseas training may or may not be a factor tending to inculcate professional detachment; it must certainly not be accepted as the prime determinant of subsequent political reactions, for there are other forces at work and other circumstances of by no means negligible importance.

In most countries a full secondary education as a qualification for potential officers is the normal pattern, but, as we have already seen, it may actually be provided in a military environment. In some countries like Somalia, it has been largely ignored as a consideration in order to meet demands for rapid localization; in South Vietnam, commissioning in the field was for a time a common practice. In Burma, by way of contrast, many officers have been educated in association with Rangoon University and at one time did well at overseas academies subsequently for this reason. In Egypt, it is clear that the extension in 1936 of the range of social class from which officers could be drawn has been a decisive factor in creating an army officer corps in the revolutionary mould. In South Vietnam and Cambodia, since the French withdrawal, a wide cross-section of society have attained commissioned rank. This is the sort of situation which creates conflicts between generations of officers, but there are other sources of rivalries. In Somalia, Italian-trained and British-trained men do not seem to have been in harmony with one another, but the situation has been complicated by the introduction in high rank of a police officer who happened to be Italian-speaking, combined with the rapid rise of another officer who had been privately trained in Egypt at the expense of a political party. In Ceylon, the nature of the situation in recent years has brought fairly junior officers into direct relationship with senior administrators and this has been a means for malcontents to generate unrest.

Like Malaya, Ceylon's officer corps is largely British-trained. The process of training at Sandhurst for these two armies continued at a high level throughout the late 'forties and the 'fifties. More than one hundred Ceylonese officers have taken this path to a commission in the island's small force, and from Malaya with its nine infantry battalions the figure is nearer two hundred. As with the Indian and Pakistan forces, the foundations of an officer corps were laid gradually, even though, in the case of Malaya, the army did not exist at all until 1933. Some of the present serving officers in that country nevertheless have a total of more than twenty years' service. By the time of the outbreak of war against Japan in December 1941 there were nineteen serving Malayan officers; at least eight of these were subsequently executed by the Japanese. In September 1946, the first Malay officer in the reconstituted regiment was promoted to captain. Initially, however, they were all Malays; it was not until the foundation of the Federation Military College in 1953 and the creation by General Templer of the Federation, as opposed to the Malay, Regiment, that the other races, and in particular the Chinese, began to be accepted. Though the officers of the smart contingent which the Malayan government sent to the Congo in 1960 were remarkably representative in this respect, and indicative of a certain success in ethnic fusion into a nation, four-fifths of the total of between 400 and 500 officers are Malay.

In Burma, the army before independence was modelled on

the Indian pattern; since 1948, in spite of the country's with-drawal from the Commonwealth, it has owed more directly to the British pattern in spite of having drawn on assistance from a wide variety of sources. The political intervention of the army is partly the result of the emergence, against expectations, of a new professional class drawn mainly from well established families of the urban middle class with, in the senior posts, a predominance of Anglo-Burmans. The sense of solidarity has been built up partly by drawing on those with a university education, and more particularly by the establishment of a Defence Services Academy in the southern Shan States, which provides a better higher education than is generally available except at the university. The care taken with officer education in Burma is perhaps surpris-ing in view of the nature of Burmese society, but no more than in the case of Korea where a carefully balanced educational diet leads to the emergence of a product equivalent to that of gradu-ates of leading universities.

References to St Cyr-trained colonels in, for example, the Moroccan contingent to the Congo, and in reports concerning the territories formerly composing Indo-China, have led some to assume greater prescience by the French than British in this field of preparation for self-government and independence. These references, in fact, reflect more the close ties which have been preserved with France in defence matters than ambitious pro-grammes of Africanization. The policy of absorbing the elite into the French cultural pattern, which prevailed especially in French West Africa, tended against the recognition of this process as a specific problem, except in Mediterranean countries like Tunisia. In the French Equatorial Army in 1948, only six out of 321 commissioned officers were African and it was not until the middle 'fifties that active steps were taken to rectify the situation. There is no evidence that territories like the Ivory Coast, Togo, Dahomey, Congo (Brazzaville), Gabon and Chad are today as well off in terms of experienced officers as Ghana, Nigeria or even Sierra Leone.

There are dangers, however, in considering the officer corps in new states in the context of the sources of military assistance which their countries have received. The assumption that the military tradition in which such an elite is brought up determines its probable political and social behaviour cannot be substantiated. The comparison of India with Pakistan and the Sudan need only be cited[1] at this point to indicate the truth of this. What really matters is the fact that in most new countries the officer corps is a substantial part of the leadership elite and that it can, therefore, take a political initiative if it wishes to do so. The decision to do so is more likely to be due to political and social circumstances, perhaps connected with the ethnic and class composition of the corps, than to a particular professional upbringing. Nevertheless the nature of foreign military aid and the method of its application cannot be regarded as insignificant in the development of a new society at a level of activity below that of political decision. As has already been seen, these, in many cases embryonic, forces are likely to have a far more pervasive influence than their counterparts in established societies. New sets of values are continuously in the process of evolution and the contribution, conscious and unwitting, of the military elite to this process can scarcely be denied; this is partly because they themselves have absorbed and adapted the criteria of other communities, often over a period of years.

[1] For references to this comparison see, for instance, pp. 56, 119, and 122.

IX

The Pattern and Implications of Foreign Military Aid and Assistance

THE ASSUMPTION THAT THE armed forces of new states acquire particular characteristics because of the military tradition which they have inherited from their former imperial masters is, as we have seen, not easily justified. Even where a substantial proportion of the senior officer corps have been trained under the auspices of the same foreign power, as in the cases of India, Pakistan, the Sudan, Malaya and Ceylon, there is little obvious consistency in subsequent behaviour. But military assistance does not consist only in the training of officers and other ranks in the institutions of the providing country; it may also take the form of the provision of a resident military mission and of arms and equipment. With the growing complexity of the pattern of aid a clear distinction between its different forms has little validity, particularly as the supply of arms is often directly complemented by the training of men in their use. Most of the more sophisticated types of weapon and aircraft would be virtually useless without such training, which means that the purely commercial armaments transaction is not as common as is generally supposed; quite apart from the issue of export licences the government concerned almost inevitably becomes officially involved in other ways. This has the important implication of establishing a preference for sources of supply where there is, for instance, no language problem, and partly accounts for South African persistence whenever feasible in purchases from Britain and for the disillusionment which followed in some cases on military agreements with communist countries.

Generally speaking, new states are without the resources of manpower and materials adequately to supply their own military needs. They select their sources of foreign aid, sometimes fortuitously, but normally on grounds of a combination of political expediency and practical efficiency. Inevitably such arrangements bring new kinds of cultural contact, all the implications of which have not been foreseen when the original decision is taken. Sometimes, however, as in the case of Ghana, there is a deliberate attempt to assert 'positive neutralism' by diversification; criticism both from communist and non-aligned states for retaining British officers in executive positions was an important contributory factor to the sudden decision to dispense with General H. T. Alexander and other expatriates in September 1961. The existence of the Commonwealth relationship has, however, served to a considerable extent painlessly to vary sources of assistance without losing the advantages of common traditions and procedure.

The extent of Commonwealth defence co-operation is often depreciated because of the progressive weakening of the strategic ties of the association. Imperial defence as a unity began to break up at the time of the Washington Naval Treaty of 1922, and ceased to exist in its old form as soon as Australasia's dependence on the United States for survival became obvious in 1942. The last twenty years have, however, seen co-operation at lower levels develop on an unprecedented scale, not only unilaterally with Britain as donor, but bilaterally between a number of combinations of countries. Each of the ex-colonies which has become independent and elected to remain within the Commonwealth has retained, according to need, the recognized right to military aid. Occasionally, as in the cases of Malaya and Nigeria (temporarily), a defence agreement has been drawn up, but in the majority of cases there has been no formality.

India and Pakistan were in a comparatively strong position, especially the former, who inherited the lion's share of the base installations of British India. Some senior officers were retained, notably in the navy, and technical assistance of different kinds was arranged. Local provision was, however, made for officer training and even Pakistan has since 1947 had no more than token representation at Sandhurst. Both, however, used advanced training facilities in Britain and provided places for British officers on an exchange basis at their own staff colleges. Political factors in both cases eventually brought about a demand for expanded armaments; Pakistan to India's dismay turned to the United States, but after the Chinese invasion of India in 1962 the disquiet was on Pakistan's part, again largely the result of the two countries' hostility to one another. India had already been in negotiation for some time with the Soviet Union for the supply of MiG fighters, but in her efforts to fortify against a further Chinese assault drew on a wide variety of sources.[1] Apart from Britain and the United States, who provided emergency reserves of material, Australia, Canada, New Zealand, Rhodesia, France, Italy, West Germany and Yugoslavia all appear to have contributed. India negotiated with Vickers-Armstrongs and Leyland Motors for the manufacture of tanks at Avadi, near Madras, and sent pilots to Britain for helicopter flying training. A notable feature of this period was the strong sales drive by the French with Alouette helicopters and tanks and an offer of Caravelle aircraft as military transports. There was evidently no political motive here and, successful or not, it demonstrates the need for caution in the assessment of influences deriving from military aid.

To a greater extent than India and Pakistan, Ceylon's small forces retained their British affiliations after 1947, and over the period of the next fifteen years about one hundred of her officers were trained at Sandhurst. In the case of Malaya, in the years spanning independence the figure was as high as 178. Malaysia, unlike other independent countries, has agreed to the stationing of Commonwealth troops from Britain, Australia and New Zealand on her soil, and during her confrontation with Indonesia has invited direct assistance from Britain. She has, at all times, had training assistance from Australia and more recently from New Zealand, and the expansion of her forces to meet the new threat, including the introduction of conscription, has already increased

[1] See, for instance, *Daily Telegraph*, September 10, 1963, which reported the situation described in this paragraph.

her dependence on the Australians for instructors and material. Her army retains a specifically British flavour through senior officers who have continually renewed their contacts on courses. She was able to field an entirely localized force in the Congo, but in Leopoldville there was no doubt as to its derivation.

Ghana achieved independence in the same year as Malaya and has, as already noted, characteristically pursued a deliberate policy of diversification, though the extent of her use of communist sources is obscure, and her military links with Britain remain closer than is sometimes supposed. Officer training for all three services has been mostly either in Britain or in Ghana, with British and local personnel in charge, but with some assistance from Canada; incidental use has been made at times of military academies in Pakistan (briefly), India and Ethiopia. There is also the matter of the sixty-eight cadets, out of a total of four hundred places offered, who were suddenly despatched to Moscow for training in 1961, but little has been heard of them or of their return to the homeland. There is a British mission in Ghana providing assistance mainly with the navy, for which in May 1963 thirty-five potential officers were under training at Dartmouth, and the air force, which was originally initiated by Israeli instructors under the command of an Indian officer.

Nigeria, like Sierra Leone, at first adhered closely to British aid, though at independence she established a slight relationship with Pakistan, which also eventually extended to Ethiopia, Canada, India and the United States, for the purpose of officer training of one kind or another. Since 1962 the expansion of the armed forces, including the raising of an air force, has been under consideration. In May 1963[1] she was reported as having signed an agreement with West Germany for the supply of medium machine guns and air force training aid. Eight Luftwaffe officers and sixty men were reported as having arrived in Nigeria with a number of Transall and Dormer training aircraft. The Nigerian government had previously negotiated for RAF assistance and apparently also with the Indian government who had been unable to help because of the frontier conflict with China.

The situation among the East African members of the Commonwealth was brought to a head by the mutinies in January 1964

[1] *The Times*, June 6, 1963.

and was stabilized by actual British military intervention, at the request of the governments concerned. It was natural that this should be followed by demands to reduce this apparent dependence either by bringing in units from Ghana or Nigeria or by recruiting a mixed African force for the purpose. In the context of this particular discussion the lesson of the East African experience is that the retention of expatriates in executive command is increasingly difficult in present conditions and that future assistance should probably take the form of military missions.

Other Commonwealth countries are smaller and have only insignificant military problems. It was natural for Jamaica in the Caribbean to make a defence pact with the United States. More important, however, has been the history of those countries which after long contact with Britain disassociated themselves from the Commonwealth for one reason or another—namely Burma, the Sudan, and British Somaliland. Burma provides an especially interesting example of ambivalence in this respect, if one bears in mind particularly the role played by the Burma National Army. A considerable number of officers received their training in Britain in the period immediately after independence, and the effect of this has been the retention of British style armed forces in spite of the intervention of a variety of other influences. Not only have most naval officers been trained at Dartmouth and air force personnel in Britain and Australia, but the artillery regiment still has a gun with the motto *Ubique* as its emblem.[1] Spitfire and Vampire aircraft have been in use at different times, and in spite of a military mission from Yugoslavia and missions to Israel and China between 1952 and 1955, a women's section of the air force has been founded clearly on the model of its British counterpart. Apart from a small number of cadets trained in the United States, Burma has relied primarily on Commonwealth countries in the shape of the United Kingdom, Australia, Pakistan and India for such assistance with officer training as she deemed herself to need.

The army in Burma under General Ne Win has emerged as a powerful political factor; the same is not only true of Pakistan

[1] For this and other interesting detail, see Hugh Tinker, *The Union of Burma*, Oxford University Press, London and New York, 3rd Edition, 1961, pp. 312, *et seq.*

121

but of the Sudan, curiously another country which presumably could have remained within the Commonwealth if it had wished. Whether the object of the army coup there in 1958 was to check Egyptian influence, to purge communists from the administration, or simply a reflection of the British trained soldiers' traditional impatience with supposedly inefficient and corrupt politicians, the fact remains that Britain's contribution to the Sudanese army was at that time predominant, though subsequently a variety of aid was accepted. Like the senior officers of the Indian and Pakistani armies, though in comparatively minute numbers those of the Sudan forces were unlike most others in new states in having seen active service in a major war. None of them had actually been trained as cadets in Britain, but most of them had attended at least three courses there and been educated in that typically imperial institution, Gordon College, Khartoum. After the establishment of the military government, there was competition for influence. Between 1959 and 1961, about fifty officers attended courses in Britain. During 1960 the Soviet Union gave five armoured cars to the Sudan and supplied on payment twenty-five troop carriers. Yugoslavia contracted to train air force and navy personnel as well as to build at the Trogir shipyard patrol boats for service on the Red Sea Coast. Britain provided four Provost jet aircraft, nine Saladin armoured cars, and three Ferrets as well as arranging for the Chief of Staff to be entertained by the Army Council—a combination of circumstances which caused Egypt to accuse Britain of seeking to reassert her influence in the upper reaches of the Nile.

The subtle balance which has prevailed in the Sudan contrasts strongly with the swift changes of front which have taken place in Somalia, where on the achievement of independence on July 1, 1960, Britain and Italy undertook jointly to assist with a programme of 'crash' Somalization in six months. This was achieved not without the eventual emergence of a conflict between officers trained in the different traditions and not even easily able to communicate with one another—a situation which seems to have been exploited with some success by a handful who had contrived by one means or another to obtain some military training in Egypt. Since that time, frontier conflicts, first with Ethiopia and then with Kenya, have brought on a Somali desire to expand the armed forces, especially in the face of Ethiopian superiority. Offers of aid from the United States, West Germany and Italy were apparently considered and rejected and, according to reports, the final spur to the offer of Russian aid to the tune of £10 million or £11 million was a Chinese proposition worth about £7 million. By early 1964, there were alleged to be about three hundred young men in training in the Soviet Union, some as air force pilots, and plans were on foot for the expansion of the army from about 4,000 strong to 20,000, which would constitute a considerable force for a people whose population totals little more than three million, whose land is barren and whose economy is correspondingly feeble. In this way, ironically, one of Africa's apparently least inherently socialist regimes will have the closest military ties with the communist bloc; it is possible that Cairo sees this as a setback as much for Egypt, whose propaganda radio has ceaselessly exploited the uncertainties of the Horn of Africa, as it may become for the West.

In an important sense, however, it is Ethiopia's relative military strength—superior to that of any state in sub-Saharan Africa apart from the Republic of South Africa—which has caused Somalia's acceptance of Russian aid. Ethiopia has strong military connections with India. After the 1961 revolt Indian officers were invited to retrain the mutinous Imperial bodyguard and they also staff the Military Academy at Harar. Young naval officers have combined Norwegian initial training with British on H.M.S. *Thunderer* at Dartmouth. The partially jet air force is advised by Swedes and Americans and commanded by a United States-trained general. The United States has provided military equipment of all kinds, including six F.86F sabre jets complete with technicians, towards the end of 1960.

The Middle Eastern countries generally have in recent years, with the recession of British influence in the area, completely changed the pattern of their military assistance. Egypt, whose army had a permanent British training mission attached between 1936 and 1947, has contrived to draw on communist sources without becoming submissive to them politically. In the immediate post-war period both Syria, in spite of her French connection, and Saudi Arabia relied on British military missions. Iraq's national army was established in 1921 and, before the institution of a local military college, sent potential officers for training to Britain and India, and in very recent times, even since the revolution, has had representatives at Sandhurst. The personal attachment of King Hussein of Jordan to the Royal Military Academy is well known, as well as the history of the Arab Legion under the command of Sir John Glubb. In the last two or three years the adhesion of Jordan to the rest of the Arab world has, however, become stronger. She trained a few officers for the FLN in Algeria during the war for independence there, and is now one of three countries surrounding Israel to receive an allocation of funds for military purposes from the new Arab High Command. Libya preserves strong military links with Britain, including the provision of training facilities.

Elsewhere along the Mediterranean shore-line, except in Algeria, French influence has remained strong. The Moroccan contingent in the Congo was successfully commanded by a St Cyr-trained colonel, and at first the independent Kingdom relied entirely on French aid. During 1960, for instance, two naval patrol boats were acquired and eight officers and thirty-three sailors sent to France for training. In the same year the Moroccan government turned down an offer by General Kassem of Iraq of four Russian MiG fighters, on the grounds that Soviet personnel were not wanted on Moroccan soil. Their attitude changed soon afterwards, perhaps as a result of the Casablanca conference on a Joint African High Command, for 14 MiG-17 jet fighters were reported to have arrived in April 1961 after 14 French Mistral fighters had been refused in exchange for French prisoners captured near the Algerian border. With the exception of Guinea and Mali, however, the pattern elsewhere in Francophone Africa is much more consistent. Defence agreements and financial ties have combined with economic weakness to maintain virtually exclusive links with France. From Senegal to Madagascar the countries of the French 'community' have been supplied with equipment, not often very up to date, and training facilities. In most cases, the armed forces are small and there is little doubt of the temporary willingness of states like the Ivory Coast and the countries of French Equatorial Africa ultimately to rely on France for protection against an external aggressor.

American military aid has not so far been an important factor in the Middle East and Africa. With the exceptions of Turkey, in any case a member of NATO, Liberia and some incidental assistance in training the efficient Tunisian forces, the impact of the United States military assistance programme has not really been felt in these areas. In parts of South-east Asia and, of course, Latin America, the picture is quite different. In Indonesia the American contribution has been considerable and may well have played an important part in maintaining the balance of forces round Soekarno, in that the army has so far been politically anti-communist, even though the more modern and sophisticated equipment of the air force and navy has come from Russian bloc sources. In South Vietnam the Americans have for some time been heavily committed in supporting the successive regimes against the enroachment and depredations of the Viet-Cong guerillas. The forces in this particular country provide an interesting example of the imposition of one foreign veneer on another. Like most of the officers, General Nguyen Khanh, who established his authority at the end of January 1964, following upon the overthrow of Ngo Dinh Diem in November 1963, achieved officer status under the French in 1954, and attended their infantry and airborne schools, but then underwent the United States Command and General Staff Course at Fort Leavenworth, Kansas. This particular course has played a part in the military education of a wider cross-section of officers from a larger number of countries than any other in the world. An additional ingredient in the South Vietnam situation is the small number of instructors provided as a result of a surprise Australian government decision in May 1962. As might be expected, American influence is not only strong also in Taiwan, but in South Korea. Here there is a military academy run on strict West Point lines. A carefully balanced education is provided on a four-year curriculum, admitting up to two hundred cadets each year, with the object of turning out the equivalent of the graduates of the universities. The cadet command organization, uniform, the honour code and the daily recitation and grading have all been modelled on the United States Military Academy to an extent not matched elsewhere in the Orient.[1] American military aid in these countries and in Latin America, where

[1] *Korean Military Academy Year Book*, 1957–8.

it is now an important force tending at last to produce a detached professionalism, is based on a well-thought-out philosophy. The emphasis is on advice and guidance, and on the provision of training places in military schools, all aimed at eventually reducing dependence on the United States for training support. Senior staff training is an essential part of this but non-commissioned ranks are not neglected. Financial provision is generous and during two years at the end of the 1950s a total of 16,500 foreign military personnel attended American courses of varying duration and standard, not only in the United States but, for instance, at the Air Force Base in the Canal Zone. Correspondingly, like the Peace Corps, her own officers are deliberately trained for the assistance role at the Military Assistance Institute, Department of Defense. As time goes on, the military aid programme is less inclined to the naïve objective of 'winning friends and influencing people' and more concerned with the establishment of efficient armed forces of reasonable size in the interests of international stability.

By contrast with American military aid, the British role seems amateurish and on a strictly *ad hoc* basis. The lack of direct preparation for service with foreign forces is barely questioned except by the individuals concerned when they find themselves in danger of being drawn into a completely unfamiliar political maelstrom. Yet the scale of this assistance has been vast, even though often on a financial 'shoe string', and its effects have probably been greater than that of any other country. This is partly due to the Commonwealth association which, due to the accident of a common administrative language and history, has at times given a considerable cohesion to forces consisting of different races. This happened in the Congo, where bilingual French-Canadian signallers were, by happy chance, able to make the co-operation still more effective. There is little doubt that the most significant element in all this lies in officer training. This is what bestows on Commonwealth forces a unique 'cameraderie'. Sandhurst and Mons Officer Cadet School, the Royal Naval College at Dartmouth, the Air Force College at Cranwell, the Camberley Staff College and the Joint Services Staff College at Latimer, the Imperial Defence College for the select few, as well as the tactical and arms schools: these are institutions whose names and traditions are now known on a worldwide basis. A young officer from Malaya or Nigeria who has been to Sandhurst is likely to return at intervals, like his British counterpart, to the more senior institutions. Since 1947, officers for more than thirty of the newer states have been trained in Britain. Some of the national figures have already been mentioned. Only the relative strengths of the different contingents have changed with the years. Whereas ten years ago overseas cadets at Sandhurst were predominantly Asian, today they are predominantly African. In the Christmas term of 1963 there were 125 overseas cadets at Sandhurst from twenty-five different countries[1] of which Nigeria headed the list with eighteen cadets. Numbers from countries outside the Commonwealth which were represented included nine from Thailand, six from Iraq, four each from Jordan and Tunisia, two each from Ethiopia and Somalia and one from Saudi-Arabia. The fears expressed in the 1920s that more than five per cent of non-British cadets would dilute the traditions and change the character of the place have never, of course, been realized; what is more important in assessing the influence of foreign aid on the forces of new states is the degree to which the effective export of these traditions, and in particular of that which decrees apolitical impartiality, actually takes place.

Officer cadets who do long courses in Britain spend up to three years in alien surroundings, which is less than would be normal in any other foreign country. If their experience is happy —and to judge by subsequent nostalgia, it is usually, but not always, so—then they return to their own countries conditioned to existence within a closed institution of a different culture. They then undergo a process of reabsorption into their own society, against which they are to some extent protected again by the nature of life in military camps. The key questions relate to the completeness of this readjustment and the time which it takes. Those who have had the opportunity to study the independent Indian army at close quarters comment on the continuing resemblance to the British army in almost every way, on the exaggerated respect for regimental customs and the continuing ritual of the officers' mess. It is important here to emphasize that, while the American forces' cohesion depends upon professional-

[1] *Daily Telegraph*, November 21, 1963.

ism springing from knowledge and understanding of military techniques and this is gaining ground in Britain, the *esprit de corps* deriving from the mess and the instinctive loyalty of officers to one another and to the regiment is still the characteristic feature of the British army even though, through early marriage, the central institution often appears today deserted and neglected. What is more, that political impartiality which is so highly valued is neither directly inculcated nor discussed and may, in fact, not be apparent from the tone of normal social conversation about the national scene. At the same time, overseas cadets' political awareness of their own countries' situation tends to be kept alive by casual meetings with fellow students in London and so on; this is probably as true of Europeans from Southern Rhodesia as of Africans from Ghana.

It is possible, therefore, to query the effectiveness of cultural transfer of this kind before enquiring about its desirability. Certainly any power giving aid can only do its best by its own standards, for if it does not and seeks to provide courses specially suited, as it thinks, for underdeveloped areas, then it is liable to be accused of discrimination. The choice, even though it may be limited, lies with the new state and the strong preference for what Britain, in particular, has to offer cannot be regarded as other than significant, and perhaps as a tribute, not overtly expressed, to the behaviour of her forces even in the colonial situation. But all this is relatively unimportant when considered in the context of the values of the new society itself. In African societies today two factors are probably more important than any others in their effect on the military ethos. The first is the tendency of one-party states, or states moving in that direction, to regard a political lack of commitment as tantamount to treachery. This would appear to indicate that the impartial public servant is for the time being an anachronism. The second factor is the continuing influence of the family which is the centre of social activity and obligation, and is, therefore, likely to confine the regimental mess to a formal, ceremonial role. The tendency of officers with heavy and far-reaching family commitments to try to opt out of what is, after all, in the first instance an additional and then, apparently, an irrelevant expense is marked. The combination of the political with this particular social consideration makes it likely that outside cultural influences will not be of the first importance and that those few whose acceptance of them is virtually complete will be regarded with some suspicion. This does not preclude the emergence of 'been-to' cliques nor instances of the retention of values acquired overseas. Some young Tanganyikan officers were reported during the mutiny in January 1964 as having remained loyal to their commanders and having been treated in the same way by the troops. But foreign training provides no guarantee of consistency of political behaviour; India's and Malaya's officers have remained apolitical, Pakistan's and Sudan's the reverse. Clearly local circumstances are more important than foreign influences even though they cause an awareness of alternative modes of behaviour.

This somewhat confused picture which refuses rationalization reduces the importance of the aiding powers' motives, for the good reason that however sinister their purposes, they are unlikely to be intentionally realized. America's professionalism and Britain's elite ethos may both tend to assist the maintenance of stability. The question arises of the possible results of communist aid. Some individuals suitably indoctrinated may manage to establish themselves in key positions, but it is generally likely that direct political training will wear off under local pressures as quickly as that which is indirect and informal. For the Afro-Asian world today, any sort of 'neo-colonialism', whether it is called that or not, is likely to produce an eventual reaction. Britain's handling of the post-mutiny situation in East Africa may be considered appropriately self-effacing; even she had soon to face the development of anti-European irritation, and this provokes the thought that sooner or later the French retention of military influence in West and Equatorial Africa, as dramatically illustrated by her, perhaps unwise, intervention in Gabon, may force its recipients into overt rejection. The pattern of military aid is confused, its motivations various, but two things are certain: its consequences are not predictable and the developed countries have a duty to meet legitimate military needs in the new states—those, that is, which appear to contribute to stability without providing the ingredients of a dangerous local arms race. Unfortunately, there are political and commercial interests which are not prepared to distinguish between the two.

X

Political Behaviour of Armed Forces
—Regional Characteristics

IN CONSIDERING THE ROLE and status of forces in new
states, it has become apparent that it is local political and
social circumstances as much as the composition of the forces
themselves which determine their general reactions and behaviour.
In other words, the axiom that a particular institution cannot
validly be considered apart from the society to which it belongs
can be accepted as proven in so far as the military are concerned.
Reports of coups involving armies do, however, tend, by implication at any rate, to assume that categories of some kinds exist.
Perhaps the forces of Moslem countries are liable to react in a
more or less standard fashion to a given situation? It is only a
step from this to the view that particular characteristics prevail
in different parts of the world; that military behaviour is a
regional phenomenon. This argument owes its origin and such
force as it has to the proneness of Latin America to military
revolution. Stereotypes have consequently developed and reality
has become obscured to the point where military intervention is
popularly regarded as synonymous with military dictatorship and
this in turn, in spite of all its varied forms, has acquired the
Ruritanian associations of the palace revolution. For this
reason, if for no other, it is worth examining aspects of the
problem in selected regions in order to test the extent to which

a common denominator does exist today. For the sake of simplification, and to avoid the complexities arising from long-term historical change, references in this chapter are confined as far as possible to the last ten or fifteen years.

Latin America

The overthrow of President Goulart of Brazil at the beginning of April 1964 appeared to mark a new phase in the long history of Latin American military coups. In one superficial sense it was the culmination of a series of events in different states which began in 1961—a resurgence of militarism. But Brazil has not conformed to the general pattern. In the first place, militarism has not been endemic in the largest and potentially the most prosperous country of South America. It is true, however, that the shadow of Cuba—the possibility of revolutions which may throw up new Castros—lies heavily over the whole region and that this arises from the slowness at which social change is taking place. The coups in the Dominican Republic and Honduras in September and October 1963 were typical and, incidentally, shook United States political circles by their irresponsibility and irrelevance. In Honduras the elected government of President Morales was overthrown ten days before properly constituted elections were due and the purpose was clearly to forestall their results. The army anticipated a new regime antagonistic to its power and privileged position and in so doing was probably accurate in its assessment of the situation. But it whipped up popular support by insinuating a communist predisposition in high places which would have been very difficult to prove. They had not even, because of the polarization of the backward Honduran Society into small educated and large illiterate groups, the Dominican justification that the middle class were discontented with the socialist trend of government. In short, they were doing nothing but demonstrate the fact that in such a state the army may well be the only effective source of power. In theory, large standing or conscript armies in which a high proportion of citizens from all classes of society at some time or another have a stake ought to be a safeguard for democracy, but there is little evidence of this in Latin America.

Even the Brazilian experience, where the army can be shown to have acted in defence of the constitution against communist infiltration, is discouraging from the point of view of democracy. Within a matter of days—by April 10, 1964—the Congress was resisting[1] an Act to set aside much of the constitution and thus causing the Minister of War to issue a decree to remove communists and fellow travellers from all public bodies to 'consolidate the victory of the anti-communist revolution in a manner which was not possible within the limits set by the present constitution'. This was admitted to be 'unconstitutional rather than constitutional'.

In some ways the wave of revolution in Latin America in the last three years can be attributed to a failure of the American Alliance for Progress with its vast programme of dollar spending on education and general social development in the area. This plan assumed that, given the money, revolution would become unnecessary. But the reverse seems to be true. As Professor Edwin Lieuwen has pointed out,[2] by 1961, when it was initiated, the twelve military rulers in Latin America in 1954 had been reduced to one, and only in Peru had this process taken place by the constitutional method of election. The political scene had been cleared of uniformed rulers but only at the expense of further exalting violence and illegality. At an early stage the Brazilian forces, in spite of their vaunted impartiality, inhibited President Goulart's plans for reform and in Ecuador the army, in spite of the direct intervention of the air force, neutralized the influence of the left-wing forces who were trying to do something about the conditions of the depressed mass of the population. In Argentina and Venezuela during 1962 and 1963, factions within the armed forces competed for power, while in Peru and Guatemala they became united to prevent social reform of almost every kind. The exceptionally favoured treatment of the Peruvian officers, whose five-year course at the military academy deliberately fosters the concept of a political elite in a country in which

[1] *The Times*, October 11, 1964.

[2] Edwin Lieuwen, 'Militarism in Latin America: a threat to the Alliance for Progress', *The World To-day*, Royal Institute of International Affairs, London, May 1963, p. 194, *et seq.*

the only state agency known in remote areas is the army, is at the root of the struggles which take place there.

Since 1961, the military have returned to power, open or clandestine, in at least eight of the twenty Latin American Republics. This will probably, in the long run, turn out to be a temporary projection of the old rivalry between military and civilian into the 1960s. The pressures for reform are, for the time being, making reaction more acute; unfortunately the countries concerned are some of the largest and most influential in the region. Elsewhere, as in Mexico and Chile, military professionalism with apolitical implications is gradually becoming a reality. This can undoubtedly be attributed in certain cases to the success of the American military aid programme which generally manages to carry out its task unobtrusively. In Cuba, of course, the armed forces played a large part in provoking revolution by their resistance to reform and were for their pains forcibly deprived of power by Castro's victory.

The unique Cuban solution of the problem of traditional militarism has tended ironically to make the armed forces more antagonistic to reform elsewhere. The tendency to military dictatorship has been temporarily strengthened because the alternative is left-wing government opposed to what remains of feudal privilege. The growing rigidity of military conservatism is likely to have two related results—more violent and extreme revolutionary governments, perhaps reliant on undesirable sources for foreign aid, and a popular determination to destroy armed forces which are seen as agents of social and political privilege. More than a century and a half of militarism in Latin America may be approaching its end. The pattern of behaviour has in recent times acquired in that part of the world a consistency which is unlikely, because of the telescoped time scale which the urge to modernize now imposes, to emerge elsewhere.

The Middle East

For a time it appeared that the Middle East might replace Latin America as the region of habitual military intervention in domestic politics. Egypt's history in the 1950s provides one of the outstanding examples of the military in politics. In the United

Arab Republic the officer corps has emerged, apparently permanently, at the pinnacle of power. The adaptation of a Moslem society, with its now archaic system of education, to the needs of the modern world demands a greater deliberate effort than is the case with, for instance, West African communities. It is not just a question of the impact of scientific and technological development but of the absorption of alien ethical concepts to which there is a 'built-in' resistance. It is the task of modernization, which most nationalist leaders recognize as essential, which in Islamic societies calls for a special kind of leadership. This was what gave General Abdul Nasser his opportunity in Egypt; the army officers had had sufficient contact with the Western world to absorb some of its administrative and technical ideas and they were, therefore, in a strong position to assume the responsibility for modernizing Egypt. In their reaction against continued imperial influence the officer corps acquired an interest in the ideas of social democracy and it is probable that they alone of existing groups could have sought to bring it about.

In dragging Egypt and the rest of the Arab world to the threshold of the modern world, the military elite has not always shown a great regard for the traditional liberal values associated with social democracy at its best. This has involved inevitably loss of personal freedom, but has been offset by the device of the authoritarian plebiscite which has helped to engage the interest of the people as well as to secure their apparent consent. What is more important, the armed forces themselves have come to see their own role in a progressive light. They have, at any rate in the higher echelons, become imbued with the idea of the transformation of society, in the interests of the masses, but in so doing they have tended to assume their own indispensability, if not infallibility, and so undermined the rather shadowy representative institutions which they have created. Sometimes this may have been conscious; if it has been, there is the justification of pre-1950 political history to fall back upon. If it is unconscious, it is due to trying to build a new political structure in a community where there were no democratic foundations and no tradition of representation at lower levels on which to rely. This, of course, is only to say that failure in this respect is often judged by largely irrelevant Western parliamentary criteria. The distinction between a military regime and the general category of dictatorships rests on the extent to which it leaves the way open to the eventual development of what may conveniently be termed some form of constitutional democracy.

As well as Egypt, Iraq and Syria have been particularly prone to military coups. They have generally arisen from corruption, the inadequacy of the existing opposition and the simple fact that the availability of arms makes the forces the final arbiters of power whenever established authority is in any way undermined. Generally in the Middle East the armies have not been forged in the fire of the struggle for independence, they have only acquired their identification with the new nation over a fairly long period as a result of social change.

In Egypt General Nasser's strength has lain in the fact that, whilst filling key posts in the government, administration and diplomacy with officers, he has not had to resort to military force internally. He has at the same time been careful to remain identified with the reform elements; he is still in the eyes of Egyptians a revolutionary. This has given no opportunity for a rising of the captains against the colonels as the colonels once rose against the generals. To this extent the Egyptian situation could be regarded as exceptional. It is in contrast with the Turkish position where friction between the young officers and the generals has been a recurrent feature even in the last two years. Satisfaction with the present regime contrasts with the typical desire for 'dynamism' on the part of those whose political allegiances lie with the intelligentsia.

Arab countries are united in their hostility to Israel. They have begun to arm those of their allies who happen to be Israel's neighbours from common funds. Even though they have so far been militarily ineffective in coping with this thorn in their flesh it may be that the Arab High Command will create a solidarity between the military groups which will have domestic repercussions. But the unwillingness of the army group in Iraq completely to eliminate the local Ba'ath party during the coup in November 1963 demonstrates clearly that General Nasser's claim to the leadership of the Arab world does not necessarily command the support of other nationals, just because they happen to be army officers. His military reputation has stemmed to a large extent from his determination to erase the old stereotype of the ineffectual Egyptian soldier. The repercussions of obvious set-backs in the Yemen or another failure against Israel are difficult to calculate but would be likely to be profound.

The behaviour of the Arab military elites in internal politics is today persistent. Egypt alone of the states affected has had a long period of stability. This may be attributed to the clear-cut political objectives of her military leadership compared with the continuous grouping and regrouping round personalities which takes place in Syria and Iraq, where complex social and class divisions are important. Professionalism is not yet pervasive amongst army officers in the Middle East and this may, in part, be attributed to extensive but somewhat haphazard communist military aid which is not really concerned with the problem of building up the national armies which it supplies.

South-east Asia

Whereas the common influence of Islam as well as Pan-Arab political motives are factors affecting the development of the armed forces in almost all Middle Eastern states, in South-east Asia the states have no such strong links. The essential individualism of Asian communities derives not only from their clear-cut cultural differences but also from the associated fact that their boundaries are largely natural and not generally those imposed by foreign empires. It is true that India, Pakistan and Burma have a history of common administration by the British Indian government but their distinguishing features are otherwise so great as to make this of comparatively little importance.

The Indonesians, for instance, got their first military training and experience under the Japanese and their national army to some extent owes its existence to the guerilla freedom fighters who played their part in preventing the return of Dutch control after 1945. Under President Soekarno's regime, with the support and guidance of General Nasution, the armed forces have emerged as the principal prop of the state and the counterbalance to possible communist influence. Their build-up was inspired by the campaign for the absorption of West New Guinea but practically justified by the continuous revolts in the islands. In a speech[1] to the Indian National Defence Academy at Khadakvasla on November 10, 1955, the then Vice-President of Indonesia, M. Hatta, explained his view of the role of the armed forces as defenders of the integrity of the state and protectors of democracy. This might have been interpreted as implying a right to intervene when abuses of the constitution appeared likely to take place, but in practice in Indonesia, because of the divisions within itself, the officer corps has been at the disposal of President Soekarno for the maintenance of the *status quo*. The recent rapid expansion of the armed forces has provided opportunities for promotion which have inevitably turned men who may previously have thought of themselves as progressives, even revolutionaries, into sedate citizens content to enjoy the perquisites of power in a country where the economic situation is deteriorating. The supply on a large scale of sophisticated Soviet arms to all three services has created certain problems with regard to their handling, but it has also served to build up the *amour propre* of those under whose control these evidences of modernization come. This is altogether a dangerous situation in which the politicians' failure to build a prosperous society makes them more dependent on the army and perhaps more inclined to undertake military risks in international politics as a diversion from domestic difficulties; while at the same time the satisfaction of personal ambitions amongst officers tends to generate an unjustified complacency with the regime. The effect on the armed forces, especially the army, of having continually to contend with risings in the islands—twenty battalions were estimated to be deployed in the Celebes archipelago in April 1964—could in the long run be serious. The discipline of the army has improved and its general cohesion increased; the successful maintenance of pressure against the Malaysian government in North Borneo could help to do the same. The strength of the army's political influence can only be increased by such developments.

Thailand presents a quite different picture. Ever since the coups of 1932, the country has virtually been under military rule

[1] Quoted by B. R. Chatterjee in 'The Role of the Armed Forces in Politics in South East Asia', *International Studies*, New Delhi, Vol. II, January 1961, pp. 221–233.

of one kind or another. The original action arose partly from general discontent with the arbitrary behaviour of the princes, but more immediately from a cut in the defence budget. Effective power was transferred from the royal house to an oligarchy which was in the first instance part army, part police and part civilian. General Pibul Songgram emerged as the 'strong man' and, with a few years' interval, governed Thailand until 1957. Eventually Field-Marshal Sarit Thanrat emerged as a critic of the regime and was given a tactical opportunity to intervene when after 1955 a certain licence was given to liberal-minded politicians to hold public meetings. Sarit's regime after his seizure of full power in 1958 was dedicated to the achievement of national unity in a revolutionary spirit and he claimed in an address to the nation that he had picked his colleagues solely for 'their expert knowledge and character regardless of personal or political connections'. He set out on a programme of reform with a distinctly puritan flavour; alongside the defeat of the communist menace, he aimed at the elimination of opium smoking, hooliganism and the worse aspects of the night life of Bangkok. Centralization, however, was maintained and democracy remained a façade; subsequent revelations have shown, as is always likely in these circumstances, the extent to which the original claims were hypocritical.

In two countries of Southern Asia, however, the army has to some extent made a reality of a purifying role. In some respects the Burmese and Pakistani situations are remarkably similar but possible generalizations about the conduct of the military there have been largely invalidated by the divergence in their experience which has become more marked with the passage of each year since the original coups. The army, in the person of General Ne Win, was first called into Burmese politics in October 1959 at the instigation of U Nu in order to prepare the way for an orderly election. A substantial parliamentary majority supported the proposition and thus the General became virtual dictator by constitutional process. For fifteen months, having warned the armed forces that this move did not imply a licence to intervene in politics, he governed the country within the terms of the constitution with the aid of a cabinet of no special political outlook. There was a general 'cleaning-up' of public life and eventually, in February 1960, the postponed elections took place; U Nu returned to power and Ne Win went back to his army command.

The effects of this period of military rule by invitation were not fully felt until, in March 1962, General Ne Win decided that he should take the initiative in putting the army back in power. The earlier experience had not only given an indication of the capacity of the army in administration but, by contrast, it had revealed the failure of the politicians to develop and co-ordinate the civil service. It had also given the military elite a taste of power and an indication that they might be indispensable to the role of nation-building. In the subsequent two-year period of purely military function, they came to the view that the effective modernization of Burma could not be left in civil hands.

The key to Ne Win's ability to isolate the army from the people has been the pay and conditions which he has provided for it. Even this did not give him any great freedom of movement around the country, which, in fact, has been united against him. In May 1962 he issued a manifesto declaring the intention of the new government to follow a specifically Burmese route to socialism and incidentally the need for armed forces committed to the defence of the socialist economy. General Ne Win has generally eschewed a cult of personality but is inspired by a passionate patriotism and is genuinely determined on the purification of public life. His success in combating corruption in the army is sometimes doubted and with the array of minority racial forces aligned against him this doubt may well be justified. There are too many factions competing for regional control in different parts of Burma.

With its national socialist drive General Ne Win's regime was from the first particularly vulnerable to communist infiltration. Rarely has a military dominated government been so prone to fission over political and economic policies. Because no promotions above the rank of brigadier in the Burmese army have recently been tolerated, officers of that rank are of some importance. It was significant that Brigadier Aung Gyi resigned in February 1963 from the Revolutionary Council; the advice of the more left-wing Brigadier Tin Pe who was then Minister of Agriculture was clearly dominant. Nationalization, especially of the banks, was the issue as part of the long-term programme for taking over all the means of production, distribution and trade. In spite of the long standing military connections with the West, the Revolutionary Council was at this stage pronouncedly anti-foreign. The attempt to set the Burma Socialist Programme Party on its feet meant that it drew such strength as it had from the armed forces. To suggest that in Burma the army has been either a thorough cleanser or a real stabilizer or even that it has enabled the country to overcome its post-war, post-independence malaise is to be somewhat optimistic.

In Pakistan, Field-Marshal Ayub Khan's original intention was apparently the same as that of General Ne Win; petty intrigue, corruption and inefficiency were to be eliminated and moral values were to be reinstated in the national life. The army attempted to appeal to the people over the heads of those with existing vested interests. The references to 'democratic training' and 'basic democracy' in the two countries seemed to correspond. But as time has passed the contrasts have emerged. Field-Marshal Ayub Khan's deliberate avoidance of more than the occasional phrase with an ideological connotation has seemed in keeping with his declared intention ultimately to end military rule. By 1962, a new constitution had modified the martial law regime and introduced a form of 'basic democracy'; since then political progress has been slow, largely because of the unlikelihood of stable political parties emerging which can tackle the problems which were the root causes of the coup in 1958. Corruption and inefficiency may have required the emergence of the sort of leadership which only the military could and did give when it took over the provincial administrations and large industrial organizations. But there was more to Ayub Khan's revolution than this. The basic weakness of Pakistan is the geographical factor—the fact of the separation of East and West Pakistan by one thousand miles of India—associated with concomitant ethnic and economic difficulties. The army's leadership is deeply rooted in the landowning aristocracy of West Pakistan, but the Moslem faith is the only fundamental link between the two parts of the country, for in East Pakistan, which produces the jute and earns the major portion of the country's foreign currency, the dominant factor is the once oppressed Bengali peasantry. Only the army could provide the security which both wings of the country needed, restrain the popular politicians of East Pakistan and at the same time share power, influence and the capital for development between the two. Nor would a civil government for long have willingly tolerated a rate of military expenditure which has over a period of time averaged about sixty per cent of the national budget.

Centralized authority wielded discreetly in the West and more overtly in the East, but generally through civilian channels of administration, has been the key to Pakistan's government in the years since 1958. The fact that the President has not readily been able to dictate the steps to remake parliamentary government on the lines he had planned is probably a measure of his unwillingness to accept the full implications of adopting fully authoritarian rule and of turning it into 'guided' democracy. The Field-Marshal is obviously no student of the history of political thought from Rousseau to Hegel nor a devotee of any modern ideology. The extent to which his approach to politics is specifically governed by the military weakness of Pakistan's position should not be undervalued. A country so divided, with long land frontiers and having as neighbours or near-neighbours Russia, China and India, inevitably conditions the thought of the practical men amongst its leaders; admittedly the martial tradition is very strong in West Pakistan, but Western alliances and American military aid have still been necessary to give the country strength. The 'share out' of base installations in 1947 inevitably, for geographical reasons, favoured India; Pakistan had not even the benefit of an established military academy or of any ordnance factories. The sense of a struggle for survival seen in the context of the relationship with India imbues Pakistani attitudes and has been an important factor in establishing the military regime and perhaps in determining its unique nature.

Africa

The sophistication of the military role in the various Southeast Asian countries at present seems unlikely to be repeated in Africa. In that continent, military establishments are generally so small and the achievement of independence has been so quick that there has been little opportunity for the crystallization of attitudes. To point to the mutinies in East Africa in January 1964 as forerunners of a grand intervention in politics of African armies is to magnify their significance. The claim that these disorders were the result largely of pay and promotion grievances seems substantiated. At the time of the Tanganyika revolt, about thirty-five officers were African and twenty-nine British in the whole force, but no non-European had reached field rank, in contrast, incidentally, to Kenya where there was an African lieutenant-colonel in command of a unit at the independence celebrations in December 1963. Pay and conditions had remained static since independence and a plan for complete Africanization by the end of 1964 had apparently not been received with a great sense of urgency on the part of the politicians. The mutiny was followed by a temporary breakdown of order in the capital but no real attempt by the army to seize power; this was clearly not a military coup in the established sense, but a violent protest against conditions, the timing for which was affected by the rising in the island of Zanzibar, separated from the barracks by thirty miles of sea but linked by history to the mainland and actually within sight of the officers' quarters. The mutiny may, however, have had more than one facet; at the time, the frustrated ambitions of young Sandhurst-trained officers, taught to regard themselves as an elite, were thought by some observers to be a contributory factor. As such they may be accepted but according to reported statements by the British officers concerned, the majority remained 'loyal' in the crisis and some were detained with their white colleagues. In Kenya, the mutineers at Lanet were dealt with sternly by the government; their reaction, and perhaps that of the troops in Uganda, was in a sense imitative, and in all cases, as well as in Northern Rhodesia, a review of pay and conditions has ensued.

In East Africa British troops intervened, with economy of force, at the request of the governments concerned and there has for this reason been some disposition to compare the situation in the region with that in Gabon in former French Equatorial Africa a month later. But there, to all intents and purposes, the French took the initiative, even to the extent of searching out the Vice-President of the Republic and suggesting that he should request French aid as a justification for their intervention. It is a reason-

able assumption that this was prompted as much by the question
of the prestige of France *vis-à-vis* Britain and her action in East
Africa as by the mineral wealth of Gabon. The series of defence
agreements which France made with the members of the community in 1960 were unlike anything undertaken by Britain
with regard to her former colonies. The reference they contained
to internal defence had the effect of imposing an embarrassing
situation on the French government, a possibility that was not
widely appreciated at the time the agreements were made. Though
no decision on principle ever appears to have been taken, at least
in the pre-Gabon period, in practice there was some attempt to
apply a rule that while a mutiny might justify intervention on
behalf of the legitimate government, a popular rising against a
discredited regime would not. This tacit rationalization and
simplification of a difficult position did not do a great deal to
further understanding of the problem of the military in politics or
indeed to help the French. In the Togo Republic, discharged
veterans as well as the tiny army made possible the overthrow of
President Olympio's regime and his assassination. In Congo
(Brazzaville), French troops were available but remained un-
committed when the Abbé Fulbert Youlou was forced out of
office. This may have been the result of a growing awareness of the
dangers of intervening in internal African affairs. Certainly the
Dahomey rising by an army only eight hundred strong could have
been regarded as a mutiny, but the final dissolution of President
Maga's government was permitted to take place. Thus the restoration of President M'ba in Gabon seemed inconsistent with a
pattern of French 'neutralism', which probably will have to be
revived, because it is likely that such incidents will occur with
some frequency in Africa during the coming years and there is
little reason why they should be regarded with particular dismay.

While the armed forces of Africa remain small in proportion
to the total populations and to the areas of the countries, they
may well intervene in politics in conjunction with other elements,
perhaps from the police and civil service, but they are unlikely
to be able to consolidate their positions and establish military
regimes. They generally lack the necessary professional cohesion
and have not sufficient technical 'know how' to be regarded
as uniquely capable of running a country. This is almost certainly

the answer to those who pose the question of the possibility of military coups in Nigeria or more particularly in Ghana when ennui or resentment against the current regime become dominant emotions. It is true that Ghana has some of the conditions which might make a seizure of power possible; it is a compact country with communications markedly superior to those of any of its neighbours. But in spite of a concentration of the army round the capital in 1961, for instance, there have been few signs of its political inclination. It has no set tribal affiliations which might make it dangerous politically, and it has been consistently cultivated by President Nkrumah. Full Africanization may in the long run produce discontent arising from the cessation of rapid promotion, but it is likely that any political initiative would come from outside rather than inside the forces.

The sporadic outbreaks of minor military intervention in African politics are not to be taken, except perhaps in the Congo, as indicating a universal proneness to the historical malaise of Latin America. African leaders today are generally as aware of the dangers of a politically conscious army as are the young officers who might exploit a suitable opportunity. The realization that the manipulation of promotion for political sympathisers is a double edged weapon is widespread, even if at the same time Pan-African nationalism finds it difficult, even impossible, to tolerate public servants who are not, at any rate overtly, wholeheartedly committed to the regimes.

XI

Neutralism and Military Policy

IF THE CONTRIBUTION OF the armed forces to national
prestige alone is considered, the close relationship between
foreign and defence policy in new states is clearly apparent.
The process of nation-building is both a domestic and an international affair. Internally, the army may be used, as we have seen,
deliberately to stimulate national consciousness and to fuse
together disparate elements in society; this is part of a procedure
with many facets, the success of which can be partly gauged by,
for instance, the extent to which tribal groups came to identify
themselves with the national state. It is, nevertheless, a process
which is still in most cases incomplete and closely linked with
the attempt by public relations of one kind and another to create
an image for the country concerned by which it can be recognized in international affairs. The real questions are the extent to
which the internal process actually affects the determination of
foreign policy and how far the character of the armed services is
moulded to meet the needs of such a policy.

The process of achieving nationhood has today been so
compressed that its ingredients are often forgotten. The drive to
modernize is inextricably involved with the practical problems
of unification. The government has to acquire enough power to
make its authority effective throughout the land and in so doing
it may prefer too much to too little. To some observers the
tragedy of Ghana seems to be the spiral by which centralized

power has escalated even when its main legitimate ends have been achieved, to the point where it has begun to create its own fissiparous tendencies. The necessary instruments of this policy, however far it is carried, are the security forces.

Without apparent economic progress and perhaps some trend towards equality of opportunity within the new society, discontent will develop sooner rather than later. This imposes a strain on resources of material and technical and managerial manpower well beyond the capacity of the country to bear on its own. External aid is necessary at a time when the internal social strains on a transitional society are at their greatest. The armed services add to the strain and are in special need of foreign assistance of a specialist and highly suspect kind. At the same time, their existence makes an essential contribution to the international standing of the state. In many new Afro-Asian countries, it is as though they have taken too seriously the implications of the Stalinist question, 'How many divisions has the Pope?', and yet most of them can afford no more than the odd battalion or a brigade or two. The foreign policy of African countries is in many ways a continuation of the struggle against imperial rule and presumably will continue to be so until 'the last outposts of colonialism' have been eliminated. Militant Pan-Africanism may be in itself a potent political force, but in the eyes of its exponents it seems to need the backing of at least a gesture of military strength. Threats are clearly meaningless if there is no means at all of making them militarily effective. Soekarno's drive against Dutch New Guinea would not have been likely to succeed without the capacity to make trouble there, and the same must be the case with those involved in applying pressures against Portuguese Africa and the Republic of South Africa, even though their positions as yet remain largely intact.

To gauge the importance of relative military strengths in persuading allegedly 'neo-colonialist' neighbours to toe the line of 'positive neutralism' is a difficult task. So far, African attempts, stemming in turn from the Casablanca and Addis Ababa conferences, to create joint commands with a common purpose have failed. This can be readily attributed to internal rivalries but must also be linked to the cumulative weakness of their forces which makes any sort of international military objective—an invasion, for example, of Angola or the Republic—quite impracticable. The neutral states are militarily weak and their limitations in this respect make themselves felt to the extent that indirectly their foreign policy is inhibited. It is notable that Ghana's attempts, at the first meeting of the African Defence Commission in Accra in November, to organize definite military action, received scant support, even though they can be said to have derived from a shrewd appreciation of the only thing which could make the organization a reality.The fact that the Commission then decided not to meet again until the last quarter of 1964 confirms its actual contemporary futility.

Foreign policy may be the means of establishing the identity of a new state in the eyes of the world or, by a series of gestures, the means of keeping a government in power. The Nigerian government's action in expelling French representatives after the Sahara bomb test in January 1961 was a good example of a relatively inexpensive gesture of this kind. The cancellation of the Anglo-Nigerian defence agreement—even though it was not greatly different in context from the informal arrangements with other countries—was apparently recognized as necessary both by the Federal leaders and by the British government itself. The essential ambivalence of attitudes is well illustrated by this situation, because what remained largely unchanged was the flow of British military assistance to Nigeria. In the military field the reduction of foreign influence from one source is normally compensated for by its increase from another. Neutralism is difficult enough to achieve politically and almost impossible militarily without a generally unacceptable loss of efficiency. Fortunately few new states are faced with imminent threats to their territorial integrity, or are so geographically placed as to be strategically vital in the global sense.

Neutralist India is only in some senses an exception to these generalizations; though her problems are in many ways unique in that she has real defence commitments, her defence policy since independence throws light on the whole question of non-alignment over a much wider field.

Unlike most other recently independent countries, India has

permanent security interests which to a large extent she inherited from the British Empire. According to K. M. Panikkar[1] Britain's legacy to India was 'an integrated conception of the defence of India, and a doctrine of Indian defence supported by a consistent foreign policy'. The aim was to meet threats to India not on the frontier but in Afghanistan, on the coast of Arabia and in Tibet and Sinkiang—but this was on the assumption that the threat was from Russia rather than China. In the British period, moreover, the army was an instrument of imperial policy and thus available even in peacetime conditions for service in places right round the fringe of the Indian Ocean, like Somaliland. The Indian army was subordinate to Whitehall, which no doubt played a part in influencing the nature of recruiting policy (Chapter VII) and at the same time determined the extent to which armament manufacture should take place in India. Like all other overseas territories, India was the imperial instrument of 'an industrially advanced power', but unlike most colonies she had at least the resources capable of producing small arms and ammunition and of undertaking minor development work. Nevertheless, there is an essential truth in the view that the British army made possible the defence of India by the Indian army; if this was not so, why were upwards of 60,000 British troops, or about fifty per cent of her overseas garrisons, actually stationed in India before the 1939–45 war?

Independence and partition meant not only the reconstruction of the army out of a divided force, but a rethinking of strategy to meet the withdrawal of the imperial factor, as well as the frontier changes arising from the birth of Pakistan. The armies of both India and Pakistan were essentially British in pattern. The officers were united by their ability to speak English, by their contacts with associated British regiments and by the successful adoption of regimental tradition and of the life of the officers' mess with its built-in codes of behaviour. Continuity was the most significant feature of Indian regimental life from independence up to the time of the Chinese invasion. The resistance to attempts to reorganize and reorientate on specifically

[1] K. M. Panikkar, *op. cit.*, p. 23.

anti-Western lines is well described in an otherwise slight novel[1] by Manokar Malgonkar, which describes in detail the reactions of those satisfied with their professional upbringing to the reforming enthusiasm of an officer who is first and foremost a sensitive Hindu. An institution of alien derivation, the army, however, enjoyed one of the few benefits stemming from the Kashmir question. The operations in defence of the territory roused nationalist sentiment to the point where suspicions of the armed services as not truly national dropped away, a situation that did not seem to be affected by the reported fraternization between 'brother officers' of the Indian and Pakistan forces across the cease-fire line.

In practice, the creation of Pakistan and the Kashmir problem were sufficient to undermine the concept of an inherited foreign and defence policy. The loss of the North-west Frontier to Pakistan meant that India was no longer in control of the area on which British policy had been based, and more recently the vaguest gestures of negotiation between Pakistan and China have been sufficient to cause Indians to feel, with considerable justification, that their defence position has totally changed. The assumption behind the creation of an embryonic Indian navy—a logical outcome it seemed to some, of the Washington Naval Treaty of 1922—was that the danger to India in the twentieth century was from the sea, and that her importance strategically was as the nodal point in the Indian Ocean area. In fact, the fallacy of the argument was exposed in 1942; India's capacity to defend herself against a land-based Asian power, be it a Japan, which had established continental springboards close at hand, or the 'brown earth' empire of China, must be the touchstone of her defence policy.

Successful defence of a subcontinent such as even India alone is today, involves more complex defence considerations than the protection of one of the smaller African states. She requires the resources and the technical skill not only to patrol a long coastline, but to move troops quickly to meet threats from channels of ingress through the mountains, which were not regarded as militarily practicable some years ago. Though the detached

[1] M. Malgonkar, *A Distant Drum*, Asia Publishing House, London and Bombay, 1960; New York, 1961.

observer might claim that she should be able largely to ignore the Pakistan border, this is, in fact, to many Indians a dangerous frontier and one without natural geographical features. The population of India is so vast that defence can also be equated with national unity to an exceptional extent, and subversion regarded as a potentially urgent threat to the state's existence.

It may be that defence policy in India would be more clearly a matter of national concern if there was some kind of conscription, but how can a poverty-stricken democratic state in peace conditions organize any effective form of compulsory service which would affect more than a tiny proportion of the population? Ancillary youth organizations, scouts and cadet corps are useful, but it is still unlikely that, short of a major invasion committing the Indian nation to war, the soldier will be regarded as anything other than a man pursuing a separate trade of a somewhat unusual nature. Gradually, however, more conspicuous use is being made of retired officers in the government services and nationalized industries. It could be that as the focus of national pride broadens and steelworks and hydro-electric schemes assume greater importance in this context, so those who have acquired another sort of 'know-how' will be seen as providing a continuous service to the state. Already India has paid more attention to defence science than other new states; she recruits scientific workers specifically for this purpose. At the same time, her activities in this field and her general security are inhibited by a comparative lack of mineral resources. Oil is available, of course, in the Persian Gulf, but she would need help to keep the supply running in time of major danger, though not perhaps in face of the only imminent possibility.

The sweeping Chinese successes against India in October and November 1962 shocked the Indians and at the same time raised the question whether the country's defence preparations were adequate. There was a tendency to blame Britain, Pakistan and the Defence Minister, Krishna Menon, indiscriminately for the new and desperate situation. It was, of course, directly a consequence of the fact that the subcontinent's defence was no longer in the hands of unitary armed forces. The 'class' organization of the infantry it is true, had aided the division of the army between India and Pakistan, but that event had played havoc with the technical arms from which they had never wholly recovered. In some respects, however, the Indian system is exceptionally progressive. The National Defence Academy at Khadakvasla trains officers for all three services together for three out of their four years' officer training, and during two of these the course is completely common in a joint services wing. In this and other respects the Indian army seemed by 1962 to have achieved considerable success as a definitely national army. The government's foreign policy had led directly to international commitments for the defence forces. Support for the United Nations and a general sense of international responsibility led to their employment not only in supervision of the armistice arrangements in Korea and, in particular, the repatriation of prisoners, but also in the performance of similar functions in Indo-China and participation in the United Nations Emergency Force in the Middle East, as well as the provision of the largest single contingent in the Congo. It is sometimes said that the Katanga operations involving Indian troops came very near to provoking a split in the Commonwealth, but the reaction in India, as far as it could be assessed, was one of increasing pride in the capacity of that country militarily to contribute to the world peace-keeping problem. By this time the multifarious elements making up the Congress Party, most of them inherently suspicious of armed force, had come to accept the contribution which the soldiers of a neutral country could make to world peace.

The Chinese success led to a reversion to the view that army officers, in particular, were too tied to the imperial tradition, and to a somewhat panicky re-examination of India's overall defence policy. The fault, however, was not only military but political. The original apathy of many politicians about the forces, their lack of grasp of the essential problems, manifest at all times from the 1920s onwards, and their perhaps 'starry eyed' neutralism had trapped them into unrealistic appreciations of the situation. Neither the subjugation of Tibet nor the known attitude of China to the frontier problem were taken really seriously as strategic questions. No roads had been built to meet such an overland threat and the result was that where India should have had the advantage of interior lines of communication she was in fact at the disadvantage of having virtually no reliable communications at all. Lone voices had drawn attention to the danger, but without practical effect. In the event, the Chinese had the advantage of operating down from the Tibetan plateau with forces acclimatized by months of mountain life, and experienced in many cases in the Korean battlefield, against reinforcements rapidly assembled north of the Brahmaputra from the tropics of South India.

The Indian forces in the North East Frontier Agency were at a disadvantage in arms and equipment as well as in human terms. Most of their small arms were old types and their mortars were no match for those of the Chinese. The political leaders had complained at Pakistan's re-equipment militarily by the United States, but pride and neutralism, the fear of the consequences of aid with strings, prevented them obtaining any similar supplies until after the invasion had taken place. But even with the weapons then supplied the Indian army would have been hard pressed to match Chinese tactics. The commanders were imbued with outdated methods, which unfortunately had proved successful in countering Pakistan manoeuvres in Kashmir. There was no one to put them straight about their misconceptions because the politicians were even more obsessed with Pakistan than they were, and the majority were unwilling to cause any public rethinking of military needs which could be interpreted as implying that Sino-Indian relations were other than excellent. The penalties of neutralism were in this case military unpreparedness and plans for a crash expansion by six divisions, in spite of apparently being able to put in the field an army of half a million men.

India's position is unique and her case, therefore, unusual, but it is not without other lessons for smaller neutralist states. It is perhaps as well that no countries of any size or real importance have come to regard armed forces as a luxury; Western critics who have suggested that excessive armaments in undeveloped parts of the world are a threat to peace may have been unintentionally misleading. As we have already seen, economic realities are an effective curb on defence expenditure. Mr Nehru's argument had always been, until shortly before his death, that it is better to fight communism by expenditure on internal social progress than to prepare to do military battle with its forces. This was an acceptable and indeed admirable view until direct attack became a possibility. Now a reallocation of financial resources has been made necessary.

The Chinese invasion has not resulted in India's abandonment of neutralism, and there is not much evidence that her friends would have preferred it otherwise. Nevertheless the proved weaknesses of her armed forces have made it clear to some that she can probably never be any more self-sufficient for defence than any other country in the world today when confronted by the hostility of a major power. Thus the armed forces themselves, through their composition and weaknesses, which might be said to have sprung in part from their traditions, have made the further uncriticial acceptance of the five principles of co-existence difficult; neutralism remains but interdependence must from now on make up at least one strand of Indian foreign policy. This may be the cause—if there is a rational one—of the reluctance of other unaligned states to speak in India's support. The situation is complicated by the ultimate truth which is too easily forgotten— the fact that a coherent defence policy for the whole Indian sub-continent is, as far as can be predicted, unattainable. The lesson of India's experience for other new states is the urgent need continually to reassess where their real national interests lie. The danger of neutralism no longer rests in its pacifist connotations, but in the fact that it leads to gestures and stances which are unrelated to practical needs. More than any other recently independent country, India has a sophisticated, professional military elite, but it has been markedly ineffectual in persuading political eyes to watch the strategic 'ball'.

Neutralist states today are primarily interested in their own national aspirations. They are, therefore, not only concerned in trying to keep aloof from the cold war, but in asserting what they feel to be their unique position in world affairs. Few of them within the real danger areas of communist penetration could survive without the tacit support of the West; in the regions more geographically remote from subversion, they generally remain within the Western economic orbit and, perhaps, as in the case of the Francophone African countries, within its defence network as well. The instinct to keep the cold war out of Africa

153

genuinely implicit in President Nkrumah's Congo initiative with the United Nations in 1960 deserved respect—perhaps more than it received—but the ironic consequence was to demonstrate the dependence of Afro-Asian neutrals on American and, to a lesser extent, British military transport if they wanted to succeed in the peace-keeping role. Neutralism and reasonable military provision are not incompatible in the present situation, a neutral nation which neglects its own defences increases its reliance on foreign aid, and at the same time diminishes its capacity to initiate international action by example.

XII

New States and the Regional Balance of Forces

NEW STATES, IN SPITE of their understandable desire to impress the rest of the world, tend to be weak. They may in consequence be unstable and instability is a principal cause which may lead to civil war and the intervention of greater powers. There is an increasing realism in this matter on the part of those countries which are struggling to achieve nationhood. It is indeed possible to take an optimistic view of the mutinies in East Africa seen from this angle; the politicians there recognised their own limited ability to cope with a situation which showed signs of running away with them and followed this by a similar recognition of the restricted capacity of others to act for them. Though there are further possibilities of United Nations intervention like that in Cyprus, the situation there has illustrated the problems arising from the reluctance of member states to provide money and manpower and this is bound to increase if crises become more frequent; it is, nevertheless, probably true that internal disorder will generally produce an *ad hoc* solution which tends to offset the risk of major conflict. This is much more likely to arise from a clash of national aspirations springing from ideological or other motives.

In the world today there are a number of what may be conveniently described as 'flash points'. Most of them like Berlin, the India-China border dispute and the Chinese off-shore islands involve one or more great powers. China is the most frequently involved and to her presence may also be attributed the generally tense situation in the northern part of South-east Asia, especially the 'hot' guerilla war in Vietnam. In this area, only the counterbalance of elaborate American aid has so far prevented a breach in the defences against communist penetration which might in the long run lead to the capitulation of the whole region. In such a situation, however, the ultimate responsibility lies not with the successor states themselves but with their international sponsors. The determining factor is not the strength of local forces in a positive or negative sense, but the willingness of great powers to provide direct assistance. There are, however, two areas of the world in which the confrontation involving a threat to peace is still a matter of local decision and will. These are in the southern part of South-east Asia where Indonesia threatens the existence of what was a "peace loving" Malaysia, and in Africa where Pan-African gestures against the 'outposts of colonialism'—the Republic, the Portuguese territories and Southern Rhodesia—are militant to the point where military action is threatened, even though the day of its effective realization may be comparatively remote.

South-east Asia

Malaya became independent in 1957 after a struggle for survival for nearly ten years against a communist insurrection which had its roots in wartime anti-Japanese guerrilla warfare. It was this fact which gave the terrorists a confidence, cohesion and vitality which has rarely been equalled. Some of them still survive in the jungles on either side of the Siamese border and the difficulties of the Malaysian government should the Indonesians choose to emulate them, as they are showing signs of doing, do not require much imagination. The existence of Malaysia, which is somewhat isolated diplomatically because of her Western ties, is threatened by a vast island empire with a population not far short of one hundred million people, some of whom have a fairly high standard of living but most of whom are near the subsistence line. Sarawak, Sabah and Brunei (which is not part of Malaysia)

have been the target of Indonesian guerilla activities and there
have been acts of piracy as well as bomb explosions in Singapore.
A continuance of these activities could sap the energies of
Malaysia in the years to come, but the real danger lies in a frontal
assault by Indonesia's superior armed forces against her smaller
neighbour. As will be seen, they have the initial capacity, in spite
of a number of difficulties, to deal a damaging blow. If this, however, were to be overt and readily classifiable as aggression, there
would be bound to be strong reactions on the part of Britain,
Australia, New Zealand and probably the United States, though,
so far, the predominant Western ally has shown no enthusiasm
for a commitment in Malaya. Strategically, in spite of or more
probably because of the position of the key port of Singapore,
Indonesia has what may be called geographical superiority.
Sumatra, in particular, threatens the sea approaches to Malaya,
and Indonesia generally the air approaches to Singapore except
directly from the north. The Malacca straits can easily be dominated by whichever country has military superiority. Kuching,
the capital of Sarawak, is 500 miles from Singapore by sea and the
land frontier between Borneo and Indonesia at the far end of this
tenuous line of communication is itself 600 miles long. Small
Indonesian-owned islands lie close up to the tip of the Malay
peninsula. Even allowing for the needs of internal security in
islands, whose varied ethnic background encourages local bids
for power if not for autonomy, Indonesia's threat to Malaysian
security is formidable; and she owns more varied modern equipment than is normal for Afro-Asian countries.

Evaluation of the military position in southern South-east
Asia depends to a large extent on the value attached to President
Soekarno as a bulwark against communism, which accounts for
American reluctance to reduce aid to him or indeed to criticize
openly his attitude to Malaysia. He has drawn on all sorts of
sources for his heavy equipment, the most up-to-date of which is
Russian, but for training purposes he is more indebted to the
Americans than to the communists and the army's role under the
direction of General Nasution, the Defence Minister, is assumed
to be politically anti-communist. As in all new states, there is a
considerable reluctance to reveal military information. Two
reports in British publications in recent years quote wildly

different figures of military strength: in December 1962,[1] the army's strength was given as 350,000 and in February 1964[2] another source quoted 198,000; there were similar discrepancies with regard to the air force and the navy. The exclusion or otherwise of reservists is, however, almost sufficient to account for the differences and it is worth noticing that, in any case, the army's strength considerably exceeds that of Britain; it is, however, questionable whether this is to be regarded as excessive in proportion to a population on Indonesia's scale. Nearly one-sixth of the army's strength are paratroopers, but the division of the whole into seven area commands tends to reduce its potential effectiveness especially in so far as the command organization is concerned. There is some motorized artillery of Russian origin and an adequate number of light reconnaissance vehicles and light aircraft for spotting and support. In ordinary circumstances the army's energies are involved in civil action programmes connected with all the phases of construction, production and distribution; this may, in fact, be a useful means of keeping ambitious political parties in check.

On paper, the Indonesian air force is formidable. There are probably at least eighty MiG fighters of various types and some anti-aircraft missiles. The bomber force is a mixture of American B-25s with the Tupolev-16 jet bomber, which has a range of 4,500 miles, and Ilyushin-28s. The majority of the transport aircraft are Canadian or American, and the training aircraft Japanese. Helicopters also are of mixed cosmopolitan origin. The navy has aircraft of its own, including British-made Fairey Gannets. The total number of ships is in the region of 250 with between twelve and twenty submarines, all believed to be of the Russian long range 'W' class. The most extraordinary acquisition, in the circumstances, is the 19,000-ton Sverdlov-type Russian cruiser with the latest electronic equipment. It is this item more than any other which raises the important question of the extent of Indonesia's capacity actually to deploy her military forces effectively. Her economy is weak and her education system much poorer than that of India or Malaya. The shortage of technicians for all purposes is chronic and there is insufficient industry

[1] *Observer* Foreign News Service, December 21, 1962.
[2] *Sunday Times*, February 2, 1964.

really to stimulate their production in large numbers. Only a large and genuine military mission could offset this weakness and there is little evidence of this. The build up of communist arms in Indonesia was stimulated by Western resistance to the claim for West New Guinea, and by the end of 1962 the actual expenditure on arms and equipment on Soviet credit was reported[1] to be considerably higher than the original figure of $400 million. In practice this may have turned Indonesia into the most heavily armed country in South-east Asia but it has not given her the technical backing to become for long an important military force. It may be, however, that the Russians would be more inclined to consolidate the position created by their apparent liberality if they could see the opportunity of thwarting in some way Chinese ambitions in the area. There are, in fact, some grounds for supposing in any case that fear of China is one of the few important unifying factors in Indonesia. For the time being, however, Russian policy would appear to be, as usual, averse to an acceptance of real responsibility in a region far from the homeland. There is, at the same time, unlikely to be any application of restraint to Indonesia, which has been given the power, in itself a temptation, to deal a damaging blow to Malaysia, even though in the long run the consequences for the aggressor might be serious and her apparent friends reluctant to intervene.

Malaysia's limited capacity to retaliate has already been well demonstrated by her reliance on British assistance, invoked under the terms of the mutual defence agreement, in North Borneo. It is perhaps fortunate that her small forces have had recent experience both at home and in the Congo. By the beginning of 1964 plans had been completed for the expansion with British, Australian and New Zealand training aid of the Malaysian forces to a strength of twelve infantry battalions and two artillery regiments. The regular manpower target for the three services was raised to 27,000 and Britain alone is committed to a contribution of twenty million pounds to the cost of the effort. The intended composition of the force included two battalions of the Singapore Regiment and two of Malaysian Rangers, one of which has been raised in North Borneo and one in Sarawak. Efforts to

[1] *Observer* Foreign News Service, December 21, 1962.

balance the ethnic composition have not been altogether successful; Chinese other rank recruits have been hard to come by and
expansion has placed a severe strain on the provision of officers.
The air force and the navy have little fighting strength, but are
useful for patrol and anti-saboteur functions. The police, which
were weak in Borneo and Sarawak, are the most important
element in internal security. A struggle for survival of 10 million
people threatened by 100 million who have bases only a few sea
miles away is a serious matter and it was not surprising that in
March 1964 Tun Abdul Razak, the Federation's Defence Minister,
ordered the conscription of men in the 21 to 29 age group of
whom a maximum of 400,000 had been registered the previous
December. This in an essentially easy-going community, is a
measure of the gravity of the situation in the eyes of its Prime
Minister, Tunku Abdul Rahman.

The situation astride the Straits of Malacca, in spite of the
claims that British 'neo-colonialism' is responsible, is perhaps
the most serious of a number which may arise in the near future
from the aspirations of successor states. The Somali problem in
Africa has similar potentialities, though its origins are different.
In South-east Asia the relative economic stability of Malaysia
compared with the poverty of the densely populated Indonesian
islands may prove a cause for diversionary war satisfying to the
military elite and communists there alike. The further involvement of Commonwealth countries in the cause of Malaysia could
lead to an international imbroglio. Already the question of
military assistance to Indonesia has indicated the potentialities
of the situation as a source of emotional strain to the Western
alliance. When two apparently anti-communist countries are in
conflict, the opportunities for communist exploitation seem to
be at their greatest. The major contribution to the military
imbalance in the Indonesian area has been the exceptional volume
of Soviet armaments provided apparently more as a demonstration than as an act of aggression. This has not so far been paralleled
elsewhere. In Africa, however, there is the possibility that the
new states' frustration at their own weakness *vis-à-vis* the
Republic of South Africa could in a different way
eventually produce an even more inflammable situation.

Pan-Africanism and Southern Africa

At the Addis Ababa Summit Conference in May 1963, consideration was given to the possibility of Pan-African action against South Africa, but there was no overt discussion of direct military aggression for the proper reason that it appeared to few of the delegates to be a practical possibility. Nor does there seem to have been any serious trend in the direction of such a policy in the year after the conference. The Defence Commission of the Organization of African Unity (OAU) met for the first time in Accra in November 1963. On that occasion, the Ghana Government, in the person of the Defence Minister, Kofi Baako, who was the meeting's chairman, called for the immediate establishment of an African High Command with executive authority over an army, navy and air force to help liberate African colonies. They advocated 'the strategic siting or resiting of military bases . . . throughout Africa' and the drawing up of actual plans for the immediate liberation of the dependent territories of Africa. The evidence is that these forthright propositions were not well received by the majority of states; certainly the conference's resolutions about co-operation were stated in the most general terms. The reasons for this are complex, with realism about the prospects of a war of liberation perhaps predominant. An open conflict with South Africa would be to risk humiliating defeat and perhaps to precipitate a third world war. At the same time, there is a faith amongst African states, which may turn out to be well placed, that the pressures which they can exert through the United Nations are sufficient. The failure of the Casablanca group's Joint African High Command to achieve any practical results is taken as an indication of the difficulties, and certainly a considerable measure of co-ordination would have to take place before full co-operation would be practical. Highly developed treaty organizations like NATO still spend a considerable proportion of conference time on problems of standardization, which, though not all relevant to a regional grouping of a different kind, have a bearing on such a situation, particularly when the sources of military and equipment are so diverse.

The conclusions to be drawn from this state of affairs are that in the immediate future action against South Africa by the forces of the recently independent states is likely to take the form primarily of training saboteurs and infiltrating volunteer guerrillas, which is not an easy proposition in a well policed state like the Republic. The Portuguese territories, especially Angola, are probably more straightforward because of the common frontiers with the Congo and Tanganyika, but the caution with which Ben Bella's offer of 10,000 fully trained ex-FLN to aid the rebels has been received demonstrates, not without reason, the lack of confidence which exists between states in Pan-African circles. The clandestine provision of arms by air drop or perhaps from the sea is another field of possible activity but the distances are great. The nearest possible bases for action, such as the airfields of Northern Rhodesia, are still a long distance from the vulnerable areas of South Africa; this is a situation which would be considerably affected by the capitulation to African nationalism of Southern Rhodesia, but the timing of this event is unpredictable.

The cumulative weaknesses of the Pan-African position are dangerous in the sense that they may well lull Western leaders into a condition of complacency about Southern Africa. But in spite of the apparent divisions between the new states, there are two significant developments of which serious account has to be taken. The first of these is the undoubted decline in respectability in these circles of the once fashionable doctrines of non-violence, at least in so far as behaviour towards the Afrikaner Nationalists and the Portuguese administrations are concerned. The second, which is subtly linked to the first, is the virtual disappearance of the distinction between the extremists and the moderates. It is no longer possible to hold Ghana responsible for the more violent anti-colonial pronouncements even though, in a sense, she still takes a more militant line. (This may, however, be due to an acute sense of the dangers of humiliation which might follow an anti-climax in relations with South Africa; this could occur if no effective action, in the United Nations or outside it, follows the International Court's final decision on the status of South-west Africa.) The real, almost inevitable danger is of a mounting tension in Southern Africa involving the rest of the continent and the world at large. The fact that those who most want to intervene there are the least able to do so is bound to lead to mounting pressure on the major Western powers who have the capacity. It might be argued that if a concern for economic and strategic interests leads Britain and America ultimately to collaboration with African states under the United Nations flag, the dénouement will be less unpleasant and less disruptive of the general peace than if the tension is allowed to drag on. At this point in the argument speculation and facts are in some degree intermingled.

The weakness of the African states is indisputable. The total manpower resources of the whole continent—excluding, that is, those territories which are still white-administered but including the Mediterranean littoral—are about 400,000. Of this figure about one-third is made up of the forces of the United Arab Republic which are heavily committed in the Yemen and elsewhere, and two-thirds in all are from north of the Sahara. Even to speak of an effective strength of 130,000 men under arms in sub-Saharan Africa is misleading. The largest forces are those of Ethiopia which amount to 27–30,000 men, with the Congo Republic (Leopoldville) at approximately the same figure, but in an entirely different state of equipment, training and morale. Of the remainder, the Sudan's 11,000, Ghana's and Nigeria's 8-9,000 each are as well organized and efficient as any and only the Somali Republic's 7,000 is at present subject to rapid expansion, with Russian aid. Almost all the states in question have an internal security or frontier problem grave enough greatly to diminish the maximum contribution which they could make to an expeditionary force. The French-speaking countries are largely dependent militarily upon France. Even those with racially the strongest pro-African predisposition could scarcely deny that man for man these forces are not likely to be a match for the comparatively long established and sophisticated institutions of South Africa and Southern Rhodesia. But all these points are largely insignificant beside the technical facts. The Republic of South Africa has modern major equipment capable of repelling invasion and some of it has allegedly been purchased for a strategic role against a major enemy power intruding into the South Atlantic area. The new states of Africa have not even the means of transporting their forces to the tip of Africa. A few are acquiring civil aircraft capable of military transportation, but not in the numbers necessary for sustenance of an operation. They have few ships and only the most elementary naval forces. The improvement, since the Congo demonstrated their essential weaknesses, has been slight; without American Globemasters and naval troop transports and to a minor degree the RAF, the operation there would have petered out. Nor are there many neutralist powers in Asia capable of making a significant contribution; Indonesia and India are the largest militarily but have their own preoccupations and lack the means of operation at long range.

By contrast, South Africa is strong, though before 1955 her navy, at any rate, was derisory. Her propagandists naturally exaggerate her strength for the sake of confidence but, if due allowance is made for this, her resources still appear adequate —adequate probably to ensure a bloody fight to the death by the white population in the tip of the continent. It is a longstanding Nationalist argument that South Africa's progressively mounting armaments have been acquired to meet her responsibilities in the Western defence system. Views amongst strategists on the importance of the Cape vary, but none write it off altogether in conditions short of total global war. The theme of the Republic's commitment in the fight against communism is continually reiterated. It is true that the strength of her navy rests on the ships acquired from Britain under the terms of the Simonstown agreement in the eight years after its completion. But on land and in the air she has seemed to react to each new development in the Pan-African situation including the Addis Ababa conference. It is a reasonable assumption that the much discussed 'communist' threat is no longer narrowly defined. South Africa's permanent defence force in the financial year 1963–64 consisted of about 15,200 officers and men. These are a cadre on which a citizen force of about 70,000 men, all of whom have recently done nine months' compulsory service, is built; they are also the professional experts who fly the jet aircraft and perform other functions which the part time semi-amateur cannot easily attempt. In addition, there are about 80,000 Commandos, which are, in effect, weekend units centred round strong rifle clubs, but adequately trained for guard and anti-sabotage duties and armed with modern automatic weapons. These are all white, and there are also available 12,000 policemen of the same skin colour with a further 10,000 on the reserve; 13,700 unarmed non-whites are also available to the police. In an emergency nearly a quarter of a million out of three and a half million white citizens are readily available for armed service at different levels.

The expansion in manpower and the acquisition of equipment took a dramatic turn in 1959—a significant date. Between 1948, when the Nationalists came to power, and that year, the average annual defence expenditure was just short of £20 million, but since then the figure has multiplied more than five times. In the budget speech in March 1964, Dr Donges announced a defence expenditure of £105 million for 1964–65, an increase of £26 million on the previous year; national security arrangements now account for 26.8 per cent of the country's budget expenditure.

Apart from the training of more manpower to hold in immediate reserve, the main cause of the increased expenditure has been the range and complexity of new weapons purchased. Unlike her threatening, if somewhat distant, neighbours, South Africa has developed her own armaments' industry. Self-sufficiency in small arms and explosives was clearly desirable and has been attempted with the aid of the British South Africa Company and African Explosives and Chemical Industries (jointly owned by De Beers and I.C.I.). Tear gas, too, is being manufactured in South Africa. Until 1959–60, almost all heavy equipment came from Britain, but an increasing diversification has been attempted, though efficiency and economy have often outweighed political considerations. In 1960, South Africa ordered West German troop carriers and, after leaving the Commonwealth in 1962, French Mirage jets. Since then Alouette helicopters and a wide range of other equipment have been purchased but Britain remains principal supplier. Eighteen Buccaneer maritime strike aircraft at a cost of £18 million have caused the most controversy and, though not ideal for internal security duties, are obviously of vital importance for the defence of South Africa's coasts against attack. Westland Wasp helicopters which have an overland as well as an antisubmarine potential have been purchased, as well as eight Canberra bombers. The probability of a large scale purchase or manufacture under licence of jet training aircraft capable of armament would also increase South Africa's strength. The multiplicity of detail in this connection is not so important as the principle, the attempt to distinguish between weapons for police duties and for external defence and above all, the general effect. Current or completed purchases, taken along with the manufacture under licence of Belgian F.N. rifles, Panhard armoured cars and radio equipment, could make South Africa's dream of a twentieth century 'laager' effective. This in its turn may be inclined to induce desperate measures but not until the full range of diplomatic and political pressures has been applied.

The Western powers have to face the probability of a resolution in the United Nations for full or partial economic sanctions against South Africa, in the full knowledge that such a measure could probably only be made effective by a blockade and, therefore, with their support. Failure would perhaps involve the disintegration of the United Nations; the choice before Britain and America would be an unpalatable one involving either a return to general chaos in international affairs or action with the Afro-Asians to compel the South African government. Not to participate might involve the loss of vast investment property, and it would certainly mean abdicating any responsibility for the future stability of South Africa and for the physical survival of her white population. It seems likely that only large military contributions from the major powers could avert massacres in South Africa should economic sanctions prove successful; no other forces could or would 'hold the ring'.

The assumption that only massive assistance from Britain and America could make effective a blockade of South Africa is based on elementary strategic facts. Only the near complete elimination of her export trade and the severing of supplies of such commodities as oil and rubber could have much success against the Republic's government in its present mood. Not to enforce declared embargos would be to run the risk of ridicule. The South African coastline is about 1,500 miles long, with reasonable port facilities, other than those in Portuguese territories, at least 2,000 miles from the Cape. To control entry to three major South African ports approachable through empty oceans would require intensive patrolling by forces able to remain at sea for a fairly long period. This means the employment of carrier task forces or, perhaps in the future, fast nuclear submarines with the latest detection devices and capable of moving swiftly to intercept vessels so located. Only the United States, Britain and France could assist in this way. They would at least have a free decision to the extent that the Russians and Chinese have not at present the means to offer to act as substitutes.

The proper lesson of Southern Africa is difficult to evaluate. It is certainly a case of the military weakness of new states being able to embroil major powers. The questions are whether these powers are able to refuse to be committed and if they can, whether the exacerbating and prolonged delay while Pan-Africa builds up its forces, if it can afford to do so financially and technically, will increase the chances of a global race conflict in which the pale skinned races will be in a considerable minority. The African countries are committed to the elimination of colonialism from their continent, but they have not the military strength to achieve it. To this extent their foreign and defence policies are dangerously out of step. The dangers of the situation and its full implications are such that the Western powers' responsibility for seeking to bring about the removal of the cause of the irritation, if possible by peaceful means, is great. They need a clearly defined policy towards South Africa and a determination not to seek temporary local advantage by *ad hoc* aid to local forces, whilst being unwilling to recognize the principal object of the build-up of such forces. The will to action towards a common end in Africa is, in spite of all the fissions, stronger than elsewhere. It is not safe to assume that national considerations of self-interest will necessarily predominate in this part of the world.

XIII

International Military Co-operation for Policing and Peacekeeping

IN A NUMBER OF cases the retention and development of national military forces by newly independent states was patently influenced by a desire to be able to contribute to a limited United Nations force such as that in the Congo. It is true that the general validity of this motivation may since have been placed in doubt by the widespread reluctance to provide contingents for Cyprus and, in some cases, to meet financial obligations, but the development of the United Nations as a peacekeeping body shows signs of continuing. Apart from Cyprus, the United Nations has so far been called upon to intervene with sizeable forces in Suez, the Lebanon, Jordan and the Congo, as well as attempting to prevent the extension of the conflict in the Yemen, but it is important to distinguish between the roles assumed in each case, in particular between Suez and the Congo.

By the time the United Nations Emergency Force (UNEF) arrived in the Middle East in 1956 the conflict was over; the important remaining purpose was, therefore, to keep the combatants apart in such a way as to preserve the peace. The UNEF was, therefore, from the first a 'barrier' force. In due course it amounted to 6,000 men subscribed by ten nations, of which India and Indonesia, and possibly Brazil and Colombia, come into the category under discussion in this book. In the Lebanon, an observation group was employed, to which India again contributed. In each case only those countries which could reasonably be regarded as neutral were allowed to participate and one may here recall the Egyptian government's objection, not upheld, to the confusion which might arise from the presence on her territory in the UNEF of Canadian troops in British-style uniforms. In Jordan, where the British had intervened to maintain the integrity of the state in the face of alleged United Arab Republic activities, as well as in Lebanon, the establishment of a police barrier force was resisted by the Secretary General of the United Nations on the grounds that there were no clear-cut forces between which it could be interposed; nor would it be possible to distinguish between the functions of the United Nations force and local government troops. These operations provided some useful legal precedents for the Congo force, but little relevant political experience. In Africa in July 1960, the United Nations was called upon to intervene within a state in an attempt to preserve law and order and circumstances involved the organization in taking the side of the central government against dissident provincial organizations. Thus the armies of many new states gained their first international experience in conditions where the United Nations was eventually attempting to achieve a political end, where their own governments often had political axes to grind and in which there was a potent racial factor.

At first, in the face of internal crisis, the Lumumba government of the Congo actually claimed to be invoking aid under the terms of Article 39 of the United Nations Charter, alleging aggression by Belgian metropolitan troops and inviting assistance only from strictly neutralist countries. Realism about the nature of the situation soon prevailed, but the opening manoeuvres had unfortunately served to stimulate anti-colonialist emotions. It is in the light of this that the effectiveness of the component parts of the United Nations force and the effect of the operation on their outlook and morale must be judged. The mutiny of the *Force Publique*, the ensuing collapse of internal security and Tshombe's declaration of Katangan independence on July 11, 1960, combined to produce an atmosphere severely testing to untried forces serving in a strange land. The Ghanaians and the Tunisians set the operation in motion with extraordinary rapidity and were on patrol in Leopoldville within forty-eight hours of the relevant United Nations resolution. Initial enterprise by Major-General H. T. Alexander as Chief of Defence Staff of the Ghana forces, in disarming the mutinous *Force Publique* was counter-manded, and confusion through the lack of precise instructions and sufficient authority set in. Apart from the general considera-tion of the United Nations forces' effectiveness, this deprived the commanders' of contingents of the chance of the really valuable experience of acting within the terms of a clear-cut brief, which might well have produced long term benefits for the morale of their armed forces as a whole. As it was, the force could not take military action on its own initiative and could act only in self-defence. A prohibition was placed on any action that could be construed as partisan and there was, therefore, no practical possibility of disposing of any group which was obstructing the general purpose of the operation or of disarming the *Force Publique*. The confusion was made greater by the diplomatic activities of the great powers including Russia and the resurgence of tribal con-flicts, especially between the Lulua and Baluba peoples. The forces of the former, the five permanent members of the Security Council, were excluded from direct participation, though without their air forces, those of the United States and Britain in particular, the operation could never have been mounted. By July 28 the United States Air Force had flown 211 sorties to Leopoldville alone, mostly by way of Kano, as well as some from Addis Ababa to Stanleyville with Ethiopian troops.

A dependence upon the developed countries for staff officers, as well as for long range air transport, was apparent. Initially the headquarters of the Swedish General Carl von Horn, who was appointed United Nations Commander, consisted largely of officers from Canada, Sweden, Norway, Denmark, Italy and New Zealand drawn from the Truce Supervisory Organization in Jerusalem. The exclusion of Frenchmen and Belgians inevitably created linguistic difficulties and, in the absence of large forces from Francophone Africa, put a premium on the French Canad-ians available. This weakness combined with the fact of being inset into French-speaking Africa and surrounded by it stimulated interest in French teaching in Commonwealth African schools,

especially those in Ghana where French classes for army officers
had already been tried.

The willingness of new African states, in particular, to part
with substantial proportions of their newly acquired military
glory was a striking feature of the period and an indication of the
appeal of international participation as part of the attempt to create
an image of maturity and modernity. The troops of Tunisia and
Ghana were followed quickly by detachments from Guinea and
Mali; within three days the total strength on the ground was
more than 5,000 and by the beginning of August 1960, twenty-
seven nations were in process of supplying detachments of one
kind or another. Already Moroccan troops under a St. Cyr-
trained colonel had saved Matadi from total chaos and an
Ethiopian battalion had arrived in Stanleyville in Orientale province. Ghanaian police had arrived in sorties of Soviet aircraft.
In spite of the erratic attitude of the Congolese to the use of
Ndjili airport outside Leopoldville, the build-up, especially of
Afro-Asian forces, including a United Arab Republic parachute
battalion, was rapid. For some months the aggregate figure
of United Nations troops was around the 20,000 mark which,
though amounting to only one United Nations soldier for every
fifty square miles of the Congo, was a formidable achievement.
Some countries, like Brazil, Burma and Ceylon, made only token
assignments of officers to headquarters staff. Others like Ghana,
who had four of her five infantry battalions committed at the
same time, Ethiopia, Tunisia and Morocco, had two or three
thousand men in the field. Nor did the pattern remain the same
throughout even the first year of the operation, for as withdrawals
took place for domestic, political and other reasons, others came
forward. In March and April 1961, India raised her contingent to
a brigade strength of 5,000 men, while, after their respective
achievements of independence, Nigeria supplied two battalions
and Sierra Leone a company.

The differing military quality of the various contingents was
a cause for journalistic comment, which had serious repercussions
on the relations between the detachments. Command and control
in a vast country were made much more difficult by the variegated
composition of the force; discipline in the last resort could only
be maintained in each contingent in accordance with the laws

of its own country. The importance of the Commonwealth connection, affecting as it did the units from Ghana, Nigeria, India, Malaya, Pakistan, Sierra Leone, Canada and a few representatives of Ceylon and New Zealand, has already been mentioned in another context, but the common experience and training of those from territories only recently free from British colonial rule in the use of minimum force and the principles of riot control had a particular significance. The Swedes, for instance, asked for a demonstration of these techniques by the Ghanaians and put what they learnt to excellent effect later in the environs of Elisabethville airport.

The main suppliers of troops, the new states, were unable to help with internal transport. Road and river travel in the Congo is a lengthy and often arduous process, so the premium was on air communications. With the great powers excluded from internal involvement the onus was placed on air force personnel from such countries as Canada and Yugoslavia as well as on charter planes. The whole question of transport was complicated by a variety of ration requirements never previously experienced in a joint force. Local purchase was difficult in any case, but few countries could have provided fish and cheese for the Swedes in adequate quantities and at the same time found a sufficiency of rice, millet, ground nut oil and meat for other nationalities. Standard packed rations of the type distributed in the second world war and the Korean war inevitably met with objections from Moslem soldiers.

Transport and signals equipment, especially long range radio, had to be provided centrally by the United Nations command and the devolution of responsibility to platoon commanders sometimes 200 miles from their senior officers imposed strains which in the remoter areas led to a general deterioration in morale. But contingents like those from Malaya and Indonesia with recent combat experience as well as the Indian, Moroccan and other forces endured the difficulties with some success. The tribal divisions and racial background to the Congo conflict did have an adverse effect on some of the forces concerned. Guaranteeing an armistice may fairly readily be within the scope of an international force and bring with it few of the implications of political involvement, but in the Congo the United Nations troops and administrators were charged with no less a task than preventing all-out civil war and creating a nation in an area where the concept of nationhood was not understood. The potential strain on contingents in which Europeans and Africans were serving side by side does not require elaboration, though it did not by any means invariably occur. It was, however, not easy to avoid when a sense of guilt arose from participation in operations in which Africans were killed in order, directly or indirectly, to protect European interests. There were also deliberate attempts, probably communist-inspired, to create discord between officers and men of different skin pigmentation as well as to discredit United Nations troops in the eyes of the local population by spreading reports of, for instance, the alleged high incidence of venereal disease among them and so on. It is open to discussion how far the well intentioned, but typically naïve, efforts of the Moral Rearmament team helped to heal the wounds; they were able to use the radio and other means for the purpose. The diversity of influences to which the troops were subjected in the Congo was bound to have an effect on their relationship with their own states, but only to an important degree if the contingent represented a high proportion of the forces of a small community. Such evidence as there is, and it can only be an informal impression, suggests a cynicism about politicians arising from the patently self-interested manoeuvres of outside interests in the Congo. Particularly in Leopoldville to begin with and later in Katanga, they were witnesses of episodes not calculated to inspire confidence in their own and others' political masters.

This is not the place for a detailed analysis of the phases of the United Nations operation such as has been attempted in some recent publications.[1] The likelihood of another operation similar to that attempted in Katanga is not great. It is sufficient to say here that throughout the Congo operation actions were determined by the political predilections of groups of states rather than by the military requirements of the situation. The ability to withdraw contingents at will was, however, a means of bringing pressure to bear for the acceptance of a particular decision. The ability of the United Nations command to act

[1] e.g. Arthur Lee Burns and Nina Heathcote, *Peacekeeping by U.N. Forces* (Princeton Studies in World Politics, No. 4), Pall Mall Press, London, 1963; Frederick A. Praeger, New York, 1963.

impartially did occasionally depend upon the attitudes of the contingents available for each individual operation. The question is whether such dependence on the caprice of comparatively small new states would be greatly diminished by the recruitment of some form of standing United Nations police. It seems on the face of it unlikely that such an arrangement would alter the fact that diplomatic considerations, however assessed, are paramount. There is little evidence here of the military collectively exerting the sort of pressure on international decisions which is frequently deployed domestically within the framework of a state, but a new kind of international professionalism could arise if the tradition of a lifetime of service developed. There are some signs of this already in civil circles amongst the more devoted members of the United Nations Secretariat.

The organization of a permanent United Nations peacekeeping force would impose burdens on member states which at present they do not appear to find acceptable. This is at least true of the financial aspect if one considers the difficulty of collecting existing dues. This is a less important objection to the recruitment of such a force than the fact that political considerations inevitably affect the desirable racial composition in any particular case. Supposing, for example, that economic sanctions were to bring about a collapse of the South African regime, the problem of the protection of the white minority against reprisals would create special problems, which could probably only be dealt with if one or more of the Western great powers was a participant in the holding force. Not only the ethnic composition, however, ought to vary, but also the types of unit available to suit particular operational difficulties. The lesson of the Congo in these respects is the fundamental need for member countries of the United Nations to earmark detachments of different kinds to be available on a permanent basis when intervention of any kind is decided on. The personnel of such units would require recurrent common training in techniques and, perhaps above all, education in a common language of communication. With the division of the world into power blocs it is likely that the predominantly 'new' neutralist states would have to bear the main responsibility in most situations. The contribution which the international training of selected units would make to the morale and development of their own forces could become a significant new factor in the balance of domestic power and might well hasten the emergence of a cohesive technologically-minded military elite. The subtle social effects of planning for international policing might well be more profound than the actual contribution to world order; even recurrent *ad hoc* arrangements could, by stages, transform the ethos of national armed forces for which the habit of contribution became regular.

Conclusions

THE ARMED FORCES OF the recently independent states are emerging as social and political institutions of prime importance. They may have a direct educational role in society; they certainly have an indirect one. In some cases they are the channels through which modern technology penetrates a traditional community. They are generally on the side of 'modernization', even though politically they are as often conservative as they are radical or progressive. Though they are seldom large enough to take effective aggressive action, they are part of the essential image of a nation, and may affect a state's capacity for diplomatic action. The key to their specific local characteristics lies in their sociological features, and in the extent to which they are established as fully integrated organisms within the body politic.

Technically more advanced equipment clearly gives the armed forces a greater opportunity for taking the local initiative—for having a will of their own. The same may also be true of improved organization and better training for the leadership elite. But none of these factors determine the loyalty or otherwise of the military to the existing regime. The desire to assume a role which is not strictly military in character seems to derive from extraneous factors, even though it is some form of professional cohesion or superiority which ultimately makes its assumption practicable. This in its turn may be influenced by the historical origins of the force, or by recruitment policies to some extent inherited from a period of imperial administration. The whole process is complicated by, and cannot be considered apart from, the force we recognize today as nationalism. This tends to override sectional interests and in new states to weaken the inclination of the armed forces to establish themselves as in some way separate from the rest of society. On the other hand, the nationalist leader who most quickly appreciates the need for legitimized force and intensively cultivates the agents who wield it, has a better chance of enjoying a long period of power, and his country of enjoying stability, during the crucial transitional phase from colonialism to independence.

The relative size of the armed forces in proportion to the population is clearly of some importance, but there is little evidence that a policy of conscription in the newer states increases proneness to military intervention in politics, nor are countries with very small armies immune from the possibility of a *coup d'état*. Theories involving neat formulac may have been capable of sustenance when armed forces consisted of aristocratic officers leading masses of illiterates who were nevertheless privileged by comparison with their contemporaries. Today the dominant factor is not the existence of armed forces, but the prevalence of political sentiments. This arises from the spread of education, the improvement in communications and the general erosion of parochialism. Power may still ultimately lie with those who have at their disposal the means to secure it, but political leaders have to contend with the possibility that the armed forces themselves may become in effect political parties. Failure to solve the economic and social problems of a new state invites the suspension of constitutional processes and may involve the interference of the military because they, as much as any other sector of society, are likely to be committed to the revolution which is the main feature of the current phase of history in Afro-Asia.

SHORT READING LIST OF BOOKS TO WHICH THE AUTHOR IS PRINCIPALLY INDEBTED

(i) General Works

JOHNSON, JOHN J. (*Ed.*), *The Role of the Military in Underdeveloped Countries*, Princeton University Press, Princeton, 1962.

CALVOCORESSI PETER, *World Order and New States*, Chatto and Windus, London; Frederick A. Praeger, New York, 1962.

FINER, S. E., *The Man on Horseback*, Pall Mall Press, London, 1962; Frederick A. Praeger, New York, 1963.

BURNS, ARTHUR LEE, and HEATHCOTE, NINA, *Peacekeeping by U.N. Forces from Suez to the Congo*, Pall Mall Press, London; Frederick A. Praeger, New York, 1963.

GUTTERIDGE, WILLIAM, *Armed Forces in New States*, Oxford University Press for Institute of Race Relations, London and New York, 1962.

(ii) Works on Specific Regions

LIEUWEN, EDWIN, *Arms and Politics in Latin America*, Frederick A. Praeger, revised edition, New York, 1961.

VATIKIOTIS, P. J., *The Egyptian Army in Politics: Pattern for New Nations?*, Indiana University Press, Bloomington, 1961.

Indian Armed Forces Year Book, 1959–60, Bombay, 1961.

HIRA LAL SINGH, *Problems and Policies of the British in India, 1885–98*, Asia Publishing House, London, Bombay and New York, 1963.

PANIKKAR, K. M., *Problems of Indian Defence*, Asia Publishing House, London, 1960; New York, 1961.

The Malay Regiment 1933-47, Department of Public Relations, Kuala Lumpur, Undated.

TINKER, HUGH, *The Union of Burma*, Oxford University Press, 3rd Edition, London and New York, 1961.

MOYSE-BARTLETT, Lieut. Col. H., *The King's African Rifles*, Gale and Polden, Aldershot, 1956.

THOMPSON, VIRGINIA and ADLOFF, RICHARD, *The Emerging States of French Equatorial Africa*, Oxford University Press, London, 1960; Stanford University Press, Stanford, 1960.

——, *French West Africa*, Allen and Unwin, London, 1958.

Index